VIBES OF INDIAN ECONOMY

Anand Swaroop
Suman Chandolia

First Published in March 2022

ISBN: 978-93-5611-122-6

BLUEROSE PUBLISHERS
www.BlueRoseONE.com
info@bluerosepublishers.com
+91 8882 898 898

Cover Design:
Aveek

Typographic Design:
Rohit

Distributed by: BlueRose, Amazon, Flipkart

For

Our Parents
and
Lovely kids
Aman
Kabir

About the book

In chapter one of the book a comparative analysis of National Pension System and Old Pension System has been discussed. In the government offices the endless discussion on pros and cons of National Pension System (NPS) and Old Pension System (OPS) is routine. The discussion is based on experiences and gut feeling of the individuals. Most of the government employees consider the old pension system better because it gives them certainty, security sustainability, adequacy and confidence. In this book we compare two hypothetical person joined government service on the age at 25 in 2016, with same set rules like basic pay, dearness allowance, benefits of pay commissions, gratuity, commutation etc with different pension scheme. In the book monthly calculation of salary and deductions were described from 2016 to 2052 with five yearly intervals. Interest on GPF and return on NPS are taken from average of empirical historical annual data. Finding of the discussion elaborated in various parameters like how much corpus of fund, pension etc received by both the employees.

In chapter two of the book we discussed the decadal review (2011 to 2020) of key parameters of NPS in Rajasthan with other states and all India. The chapters go through comparative analysis of various key parameters of NPS like number of subscribers, contribution and uploadation of funds, uploadation of legacy, Asset Under Management (AUM), withdrawal request received to request processed and total amount of withdrawals, Annuity Service Provider (ASP) payment process and pendency. All the data are analyzed in detailed.

In chapter three of the book the author analyzed how should be the Institutional framework of new generation of tax intelligence through E-networking and discussed state of art institution of State

Investigation Bureau (SIB). In the federal structure of governance it is very important that state governments are get through with the centre and other state governments for modernization and information sharing. State governments focus on online system to cope with central government online and digitization process. The system of vigilance and intelligence over revenue leakage cannot be based only on old system of informants and physical interventions. To improvise the system at state level a new institution is required to manage, integrate and share financial information with stakeholder departments of centre and state government.

The fourth chapter of the book explained Wagonomics after the breakthrough of demonetization. It analyzed how workers engaged in unorganized sector are facing deep trouble after demonetization. The impact of economic daunting on micro and small industries drastically spillover on unskilled or semi-skilled through wage cut to job cut. The three main mile stone policy decisions in recent Indian economy which totally destroy the nitty gritty of wagonomics in India are Demonetization, Goods and Service Tax (GST) and Lockdown. The impact of each incident is different on the socio-economic conditions of the daily wage earner, migrant workers and marginalized workers. Its effects are analyzed in unique way of discussion which is categorized in three zones namely Red zone, Grey zone and Brown zone.

In the last chapter we examine the impact of e-banking system in India. The chapters go through in detailed manners and instruments of digital payment in recent past. In India, the digital revolution has led to the surge of internet users in the country. The reference period for the study from 2015-16 to 2018-19 traditional payments systems like RTGS, NEFT, Card payments, prepaid instruments etc were on upward or stable trends in respect of volume, value or per transaction value, but after 2018-19 the percentage share and YoY growth were shrinking in above mentioned payment systems and simultaneously mobile based payment instruments such as UPI, IMPS, NETC gained weight in volume of transaction, value of transaction and per transaction value. The growing relevance of e-banking is due to digital revolution and surge of internet users in the country. The study reveals that covid-19 pandemic has given another biggest thrust to online banking in the country due to uncertain lockdown people make their transactions through online and therefore, there was a tremendous surge of e-banking users in 2020-21 within the country. The study concludes that easy and affordable internet excess with cheap smart phone benefited the e-banking ecosystem.

Peer Opinion on different chapters of Vibes of Indian Economy

On Institutional framework of State Investigation Bureau- The book titled as Vibes of Indian Economy has a specific chapter on State Investigation Bureau. The authors have rightly identified collection and collation of the information of various revenue generating departments of state governments and effective use of such information in generating revenue as a very pertinent issue which needs to be addressed by the respective state governments. The authors have not only emphasized the need of collection and collation of relevant information, but also suggested an institutional framework and organizational structure to deal with the issue by a nodal agency named as State Investigation Bureau. The state governments should give a serious thought on the suggestions of the authors, one of whom is heading such nodal agency in Rajasthan carrying out some of the tasks suggested in the chapter.

Sanjay Dhariwal, Indian Revenue Service

On Wagonomics after breakthrough - A very well written paper on the impact and ways forward after demonetization and other setbacks to workers' economy. I really liked the directness with which you have described the three stages of massive impact – demonetization, GST and then COVID. You're quite correct in noting that this cumulative impact runs deep – both at the household level of the workers and also in the lower wrung of the working class economy. It is surprising how neo-liberal economists and policy makers are now saying that the economy is fully recovered while we know that the working poor are still to recover from this three pronged damage to their livelihood.

On Comparative study of NPS and OPS - The chapter on OPS vs. NPS critically analyzes a much-debated issue of our times viz. which type of pension scheme is better for a government employee – the old pension system or the more recent national pension scheme. While views are sharply divided on this important issue, this chapter presents a masterful analytical comparison to show that the answer is nuanced, complex and conditional. The authors analyze a vast amount of data and simulate the scenarios in which either of the two may be better. This chapter will be of immense benefit to the subscribers, regulators and scholars of pension schemes in India.

On Institutional framework of State Investigation Bureau- The chapter on State Investigation Bureau describes the framework for a new state institution for efficient management of revenue data by harnessing the power of big data and technology. The authors have laid out a complete roadmap for establishment of such an institution with its needs, scope, responsibilities, organizational structure and workflow. The proposed tools such as the revenue evasion petition, suspicious intelligence report, incentive scheme for informers etc. can prove to be a valuable addition to the government's revenue intelligence machinery. Practitioners and policymakers will definitely benefit by reflecting on the suggestions provided in this chapter.

On Impact of e-Banking system in India- The genesis of e-Banking and its importance in current scenario with statics and usage has been elaborated in perspective. The reading is lucid with so much information and analysis. Overall a great read for generalists as well as specialists.

Renu Lata, Indian Economic Service

On Comparative study of NPS and OPS-Valuable research on a critical topic on contractual savings, relevant for both the common man, to weigh and understand the kind of long-term commitment while opting for savings and the cover, and for policy makers, to understand the gap that needs to be addressed while formulating policy keeping in view citizens' benefit.

Vanlalruata Fanai, Resident Representative at Singapore, Export-Import Bank of India

On Comparative study of NPS and OPS- Comparison of NPS and OPS in the book is a fresh contribution to literature on retirement benefits. Using complex forecasting and modeling, the book has demonstrated - quite counter-intuitively - that benefits from NPS could be more than OPS at retirement, under certain circumstances. The book has demonstrated that NPS is actually a beneficial scheme, although it may not give the kind of security that OPS gives. At the same time, the book provides pertinent recommendations for rationalization and reform of the NPS scheme. I am sure that readers will find it immensely useful.

Smarak Swain, Indian Revenue Service

OPS vs. NPS

A comparison of benefits under Old Pension
System and National Pension System

Contents

A comparative analysis of National Pension System and Old pension System

Introduction

After the introduction of the National Pension System (NPS), it was argued that this scheme will give less burden to the Government, in other words, employees who joined after 01.01.2004 think that this scheme is not better than the old pension system. In this regard, most of the employees' unions are have been campaigning to restore the old pension system (OPS) after the implementation of the National Pension System in the year 2004.

Most of the government employees consider the old pension system better because it gives them certainty, security, sustainability, adequacy, and confidence. Before the implementation of NPS in January 2004, when a government employee retired, his pension was fixed equal to 50 percent of his last salary. Whether there is a 40-year service in OPS or 10 years, the amount of pension was decided by the last salary. It was a definite benefit scheme. In contrast, NPS is a Definitive Contribution Pension Scheme, that is, the pension amount depends on the number of years the job has been done and the annuity amount. A fixed amount is contributed every month under NPS. On retirement, 60 percent of the total amount can be withdrawn in a lump sum and the remaining 40 percent has to be purchased from the insurance company's annuity plan, on which the return on the corpus amount is given as pension every month.

Both OPS and NPS are completely different pension systems. The basic difference between the old and the new scheme is that while the earlier system was defined, the new one is based on investment returns along with accumulations.

At this juncture, it is very important to know what is the difference between the two pension systems and what are the benefits to the government employees in the National Pension System . Whether NPS has faith or will gain faith in the future just as OPS, which had certainty, security, sustainability, adequacy, and confidence. Which scheme is better and what are the areas where improvement is needed? It is necessary to be aware of the circumstances under which NPS can give better returns.

National Pension System was introduced in which a defined contributory pension has been implemented for all the Government servants appointed on and after 01.01.2004. As per the guidelines, every employee must contribute 10 percent of basic pay plus dearness allowance every month from salary and equal contribution or as may be decided by the regulator is to be made by the state government.

After 17 years of the implementation of NPS, we have the necessary data to analyze which scheme is better in which area. For this, let's assume that two employees joined government service on 01.012016 and one opted for the old pension system and the other opted for the National Pension System with certain assumptions. In this article, we observe the performance of OPS and NPS during employee's service and also after superannuation.

Assumptions and considerations for comparison of NPS and OPS

I. Employee joined service at the age of 25.

II. An employee joins the state government service on 01 January 2016.

III. For the first time, the basic pay of January 2016 is taken.

IV. Dearness allowance at the rate of 3% has been included in the calculation in January and 5% in July every year.

V. A 3% annual increment has been imposed in July every year.

VI. The fixation as per the recommendation of Pay Commission every 10 years has also been considered and is estimated approximately based on the last pay commission in force in the state, which is given in the year 2016.

VII. That being said, 2.5 times the employee's salary has been fixed to that of January 2016, which is the last pay commission in force in the state.

VIII. Dearness allowance has been reduced to zero at the time of fixation of pay commission.

IX. In this calculation, if an employee belongs to All India Services (AIS), then the state contribution for his NPS is considered at the rate of 14% from the year 2019-20. The rate of state contribution is being increased by 2% in every Pay Commission payable after 01.04.2016

X. In this calculation, if an employee retires as per the old pension regime, then the amount (at the time of settlement) has been calculated based on the prevailing interest rate in the calculation of GPF. In this calculation, the rate of interest on GPF each year has been deducted at the rate of 0.1% in the following years according to the previous trends with an assumption of minimum at 6% interest.

XI. If an employee has been appointed in the state service on or after January 2016, then the average annual rate of return has been estimated at the rate of 9.85% every year based on the average returns during the last 10 years of his service (2012-2021).

XII. The payable benefits in the old pension system (OPS) and National Pension System (NPS) have been calculated according to the current prescribed benefits of the state government.

XIII. In the National Pension System (NPS), the pension calculation has been done based on Rs 750/- per lakh per month.

Basic Pay Calculation

(i) For the first time, the basic pay of January 2016 has been taken.

(ii) After this, 3% dearness allowance has been included in the calculation from January every year and 5% in the month of July.

(iii) For salary increase, 3% annual increment has been imposed in the month of July.

(iv) The pay commission has also been included in the calculation every 10 years, in which the salary given in January of the year of fixation of the pay commission is approximately on the basis of the last pay commission in force in the state, which is given in the year 2016. That being said, 2.5 times his salary has been fixed.

(v) Below the chart depicts the growth of 5 years of interval. (Derived from the annual data of 2016 to 2051)

MONTH	BASIC	D.A.	G. TOTAL	Deduction @10%
Jan'16	56100	1683	57783	5778
Jul'21	65200	32256	99456	9945.6
Jan'26	184000	5520	189520	18952
Jul'31	213600	105648	325748	32574.8
Jan'36	602000	18060	620060	62006
Jul'41	698200	345216	1064416	106441.6
Jan'46	1965000	58950	2023950	202395
Jul'51	2278300	1126416	3473116	347311.6

The table given above showcases the salary calculation over the years on a five-year gap. It is visible that the basic salary increases each year and the amount of increase in basic salary becomes more with each Pay Commission. A person who joins the AIS service in the year 2016, gets a basic salary of Rs. 56,100 and at the time of retirement, his basic salary grows to Rs. 22,78,300 which is roughly 40 times the initial basic salary. Similarly, the Gross Salary that includes basic and the DA amount becomes 60 times more than the initial gross salary of Rs. 57,783.

The charts given below depict the growth trend in Basic salary and Gross salary over years.

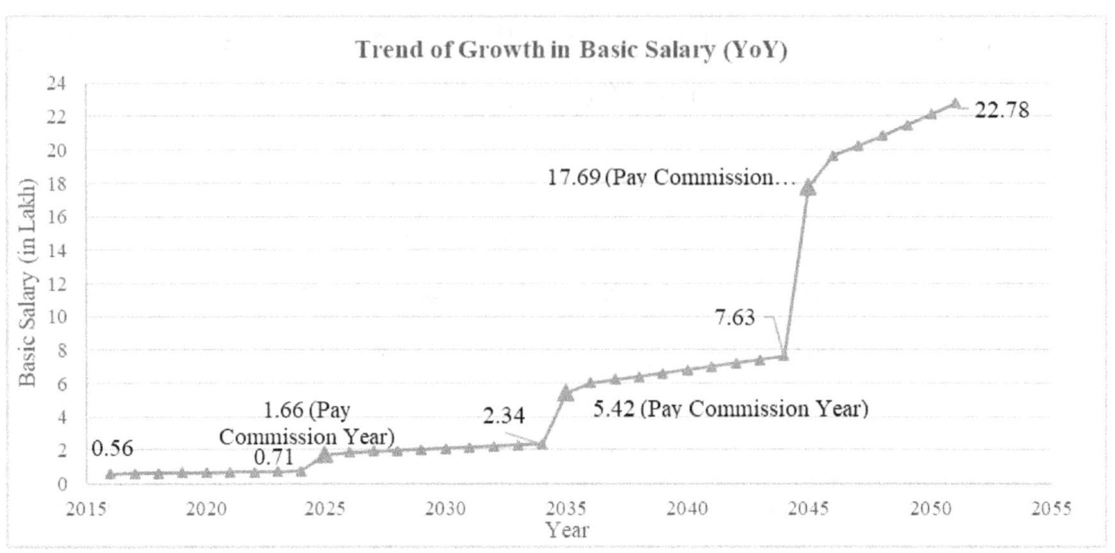

The big jump shown in the above chart is based online the years when every 10 years pay commission was implemented. The employee enjoyed 03 pay commission (2025, 2035, 2045) hikes during his service. Total salary stood up from ₹ 57783 to ₹ 3473116, which is 60 times of initial salary.

Calculation of GPF under Old pension system Employee

In this calculation, if the employee retires as per the old pension regime, then the amount (at the time of settlement) has been calculated based on the prevailing interest rate in the calculation of GPF. In this calculation, the rate of interest on GPF each year has been deducted at the rate of 0.1% in the following years according to the previous trends with an estimation of a minimum of 6% interest.

The estimation of GPF interest rates has been statistically forecasted based on the historical growth pattern of interest rates from the financial year 1980-81 to 2020-21. In the diagram given below, it can be observed that the GPF interest rate will remain around 6% if a general macroeconomic factor does not become adverse.

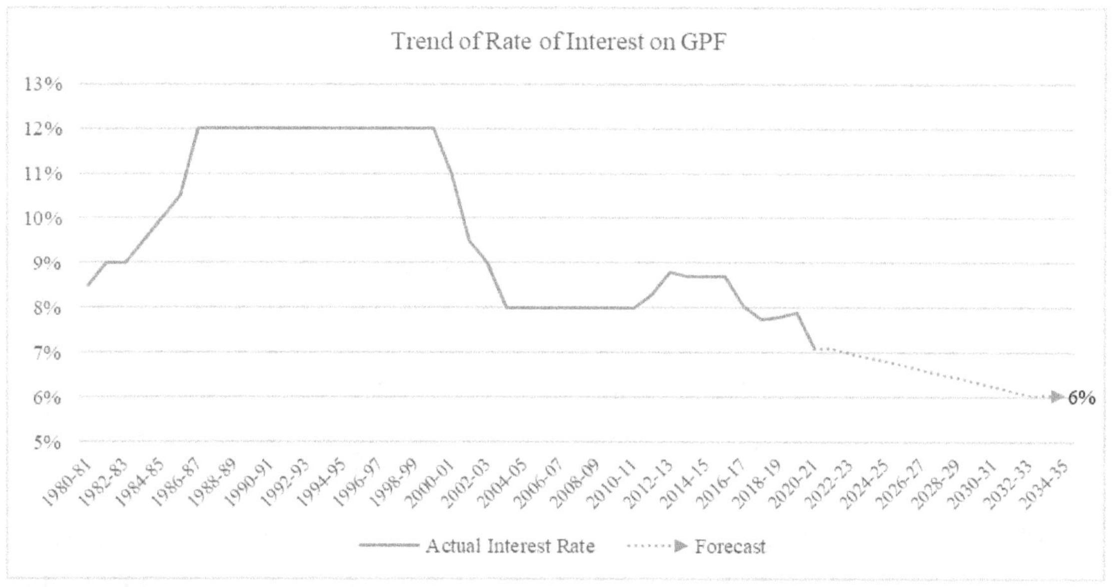

Based on the factors mentioned above, an exercise for the calculation of the GPF amount has been done. The table given below depicts the growth of GPF amount at 5 years of interval. (Derived from the annual data of 2016 to 2051).

Year	Opening Balance	Emp GPF contribution	Interest	Total
2016-2017	0	74037	3190	77227
2020-2021	400737	108375	32558	541670
2025-2016	1322921	177468	97443	1597832
2030-2031	3350479	355015	226554	3932048
2035-2036	6964041	580386	435364	7979791
2040-2041	14225161	1160525	1187552	16573238
2045-2046	28698849	1894203	1779115	32372167
2051-2052	61589290	4103195	3827259	69519744

A diagram depicting the growth of GPF amount over the years has been given below:

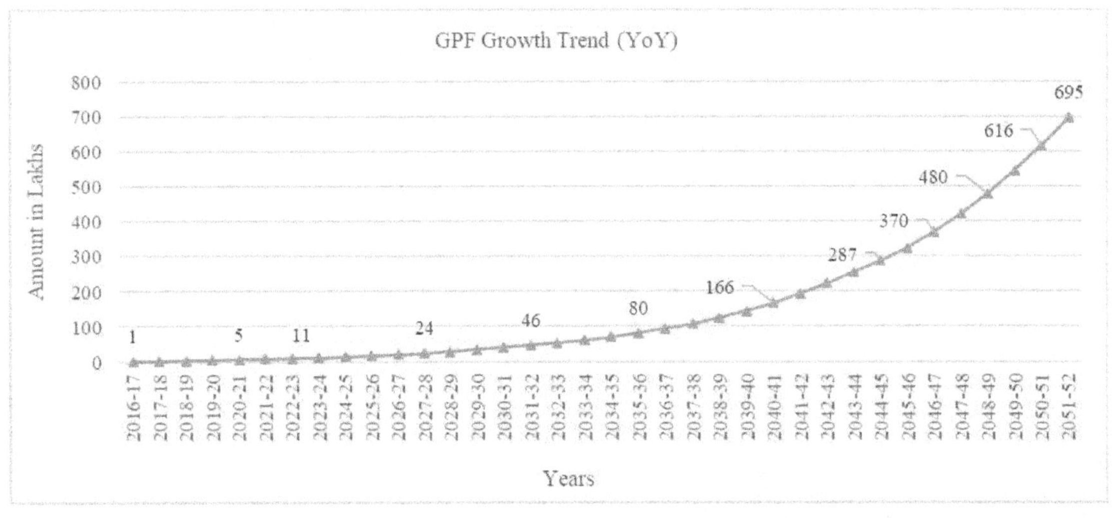

It is clear that at the time of retirement in the year 2051, an employee who joined in 2016 will get Rs 6.95 crore as the final GPF claim amount.

Calculation of corpus under NPS Employee:

If an employee has been appointed in the state service on or after January 2016, then the average annual rate of return in future service is estimated at the rate of 9.85% every year. The rate of return on NPS corpus in the future is calculated on the actual average rate of returns in the past 10 years i.e., from FY 2012-13 to FY 2021-22 as shown in the diagram given below:

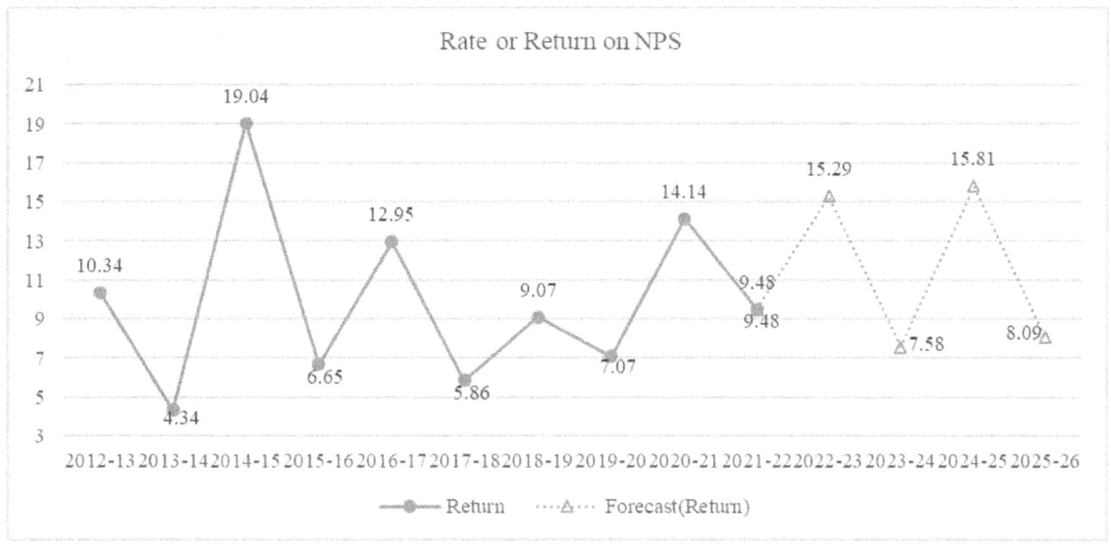

Fluctuation in the average rate of return will be narrowed down in the future since total corpus under NPS (central, State, and other schemes) will have sharply increased. And rules and regulations of NPS are improvised every year.

The table below provides a calculation of NPS on a year-on-year basis, in the case of an employee joining the AIS services in the year 2016. The table given below is prepared on a five-year interval starting from 2016-2017 to the year 2051-2052.

Year	Opening Balance	Emp contribution	Govt contribution	Interest	Total
2016-2017	0	74,037	74,037	7,759	1,55,833
2020-2021	8,74,273	1,08,375	1,51,725	99,786	12,34,159
2025-2026	33,49,691	1,77,468	2,48,455	3,51,054	41,26,668
2030-2031	95,56,162	3,55,015	5,68,024	9,89,793	1,14,68,994
2035-2036	2,22,06,300	5,80,386	9,28,618	22,62,109	2,59,77,413
2040-2041	5,03,19,964	11,60,525	20,88,945	51,27,302	5,86,96,736
2045-2046	10,48,36,612	18,94,203	34,09,565	1,05,89,265	12,07,29,645
2051-2052	25,30,62,423	41,03,195	82,06,390	2,55,76,264	29,09,48,272

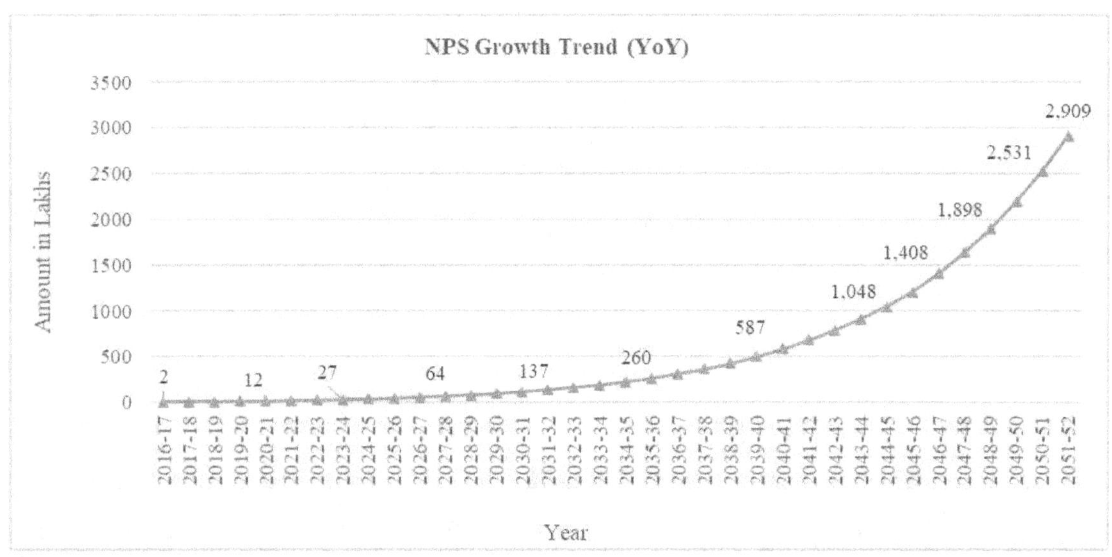

From the above diagram, it can be observed that an employee who joins his services in the year 2016 under NPS, gets a sum of Rs. 29.09 crores upon his retirement in 2051. At the time of retirement, the employee can withdraw 60% of his funds. The remaining 40% fund has to be reinvested for pension with Annuity Service Provider (ASPs). This way, the withdrawal amount and reinvestment amount can be bifurcated as given in the following table:

Total fund at the time of retirement	Rs. 29.09 Cr
60% amount (Withdrawal)	Rs. 17.46 Cr
40% amount (Reinvestment for Pension)	Rs. 11.64 Cr

Returns on NPS

At present, central and state government NPS funds are being allocated to three Pension Funds (PFS) viz SBI Pension Funds Private Limited, UTI Retirement Solutions Limited, and LIC Pension Fund Limited which are managed and invested by each pension fund as per investment guidelines issued by PFRDA.

Allocation of Assets in the central and state government Sector Maximum Exposure Limits are defined as per PFRDA rules are as under-

I. Government Securities & related investments: 55 percent

II. Debt Instruments & Related investments: 45 percent

III. Asset-backed, trust structured & Miscellaneous investments: 5 percent

IV. Short term debt instruments & related investments: 10 percent

V. Equity & related investments: 15 percent.

Further, from 2019 Government subscribers are free to choose any one of the pension funds including private sector pension funds. They could change their option once a year. From 2019 Government employees also have the freedom to choose the investment pattern given by PFRDA. Following are the investment patterns-

I. Existing scheme in which funds are allocated by the PFRDA among three Public Sector Undertaking fund managers based on their past performance by the guidelines of PFRDA for

Government employees shall continue as the default scheme for both existing and new subscribers.

II. Government employees who prefer a fixed return with a minimum amount of risk shall be given an option to invest 100% of the funds in Government securities (Scheme G)

III. Government employees who prefer higher returns shall be given the options of the following two life-cycle based schemes:

a. Conservative life cycle fund with maximum exposure to equity capped at 25% - LC-25

b. Moderate life cycle fund with maximum equity exposure capped at 50% - LC-50. The Government subscribers under NPS may choose one of the above investments.

Considering allocation of assets of central and state government employees, maximum exposure limits are defined in the rules which are summarized in two categories-

Government securities, Debt investments, Asset backed and Short-term debt investments	85%
Equity & related investments	15%

Pension fund managers invested employees' corpus in Government securities, Debt investments, Asset backed and Short-term debt investments for 85 per cent of the total investments. Rest 15 per cent corpus invested in equity and related investments. The general public perception about NPS is that it is related to market risks and therefore, there is a sense of hesitance in opting for it. For better understanding of the investment pattern and average rate of return, a statistical study of the growth status of government backed investments and equity related investment has been done.

Understanding the yields on short term and long-term investments in G-Sec and debt funds

As mentioned above, the government offers opportunities for long term and short-term investments in G-Sec, debt funds, bonds etc. on which it offers different rates of interest. The rate of interest for short term, mid- term and long term are declared prior to the investments on the basis of investment period and type of investment, which is also termed as 'Term to Maturity'. The fixed investments in government schemes have a steady return over years and offer guaranteed returns. It is worth mentioning that the 85% of the amount of NPS that goes into these government schemes are safe, reliable and profitable due to its nature of guaranteed returns. In the financial year 2021-22, the government has declared an interest rate of 3.87% in case of short-term investment for one year and goes up to 7.02% for long term investment for 30 years. In most of the cases, NPS investments are long term and attract maximum rate of interest.

An analysis of the existing rate of returns of fixed government investments has been done. The graph given below presents the actual government yield from FY 1996-97 to FY 2021-22.

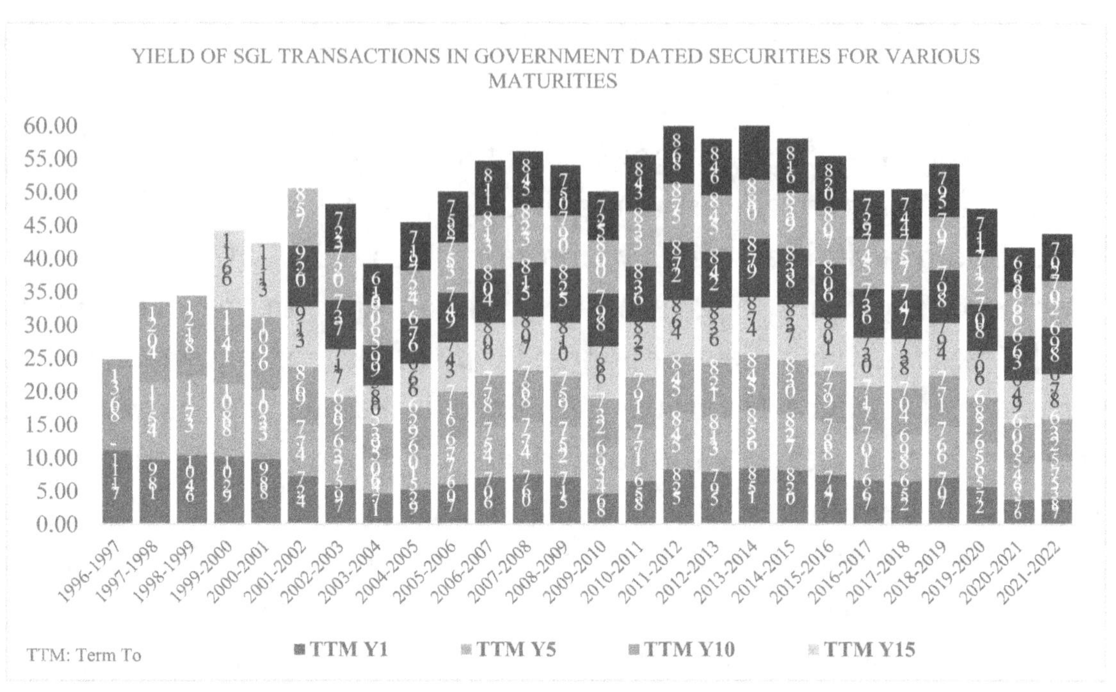

From the graph given above, it is evident that the rate of returns in long term investments such as for 20 years and above, the rate of interest has been more than seven percent till the financial year 2019-20. In the year 2020-21 the rate of interest has slightly dropped which is possibly due to the Covid pandemic. In the current financial year 2021-22, the rate of returns has increased and is around 7%, possibly on account of a reviving economy. It is also worth emphasizing that the rate of interest on long term investment has no drastic impact despite a world-wide covid pandemic.

A statistical analysis of the rate of returns, in case of long-term government investment, with a purpose to forecast the percentage yield has been done and presented in the diagram given below:

The forecasting done for rate of interest on 20 years investment shows that it will have a decreasing trend and will be steady around 5.5%. It can be understood that for long term investments for more than 20 years, it will always be more than 5.5%.

Understanding Equity & related investments of NPS fund

The pension fund in NPS is invested into government securities and equities in a percentage share of 85% and 15%. The 15% share of the funds is invested in the Large Cap segment in the equity market. According to SEBI's definition, top 100 stocks by market cap come under the large-cap segment.

	PORTFOLIO AVG MCAP (₹ CR)	LARGE CAP ALLOCATION (%)
LIC Pension Fund	1,85,329	95.9
SBI Pension Fund	2,07,578	95.4
Kotak Pension Fund	2,49,239	94.3
ICICI Prudential Pension Fund	1,59,385	94.2
Birla Sun Life Pension Scheme	2,43,525	94.0
HDFC Pension Fund	1,55,650	92.4
UTI Retirement Solutions	1,97,691	92.3

Given the current investment restrictions; NPS equity portfolios across fund managers have a heavy large-cap bias. All pension funds have more than 90% of the equity corpus in this segment. Market capitalization refers to the total number of outstanding shares of a company in the market multiplied by the current price of each share. It is a measure of the estimated valuation of a company. Large-cap companies are businesses that are well-established and have a significant market share. Large-cap companies have market caps of Rs 20,000 crore or more. These companies dominate the industry and are very stable. They hold themselves well in times of recession or during any other negative event. Besides, they have usually been functioning for decades and have good reputations. These stocks are less volatile in comparison to mid-cap and small-cap stocks. The lower volatility makes them less risky. In this manner, the 15% amount of NPS is also a profitable and sustainable investment which has very little risk of loss.

The graph given below presents a historical and forecasted performance of S&P BSE 100 Large Cap stocks. It is clear that the stocks have solid and steady growth in the years to come. This makes the investments risk-free and profitable.

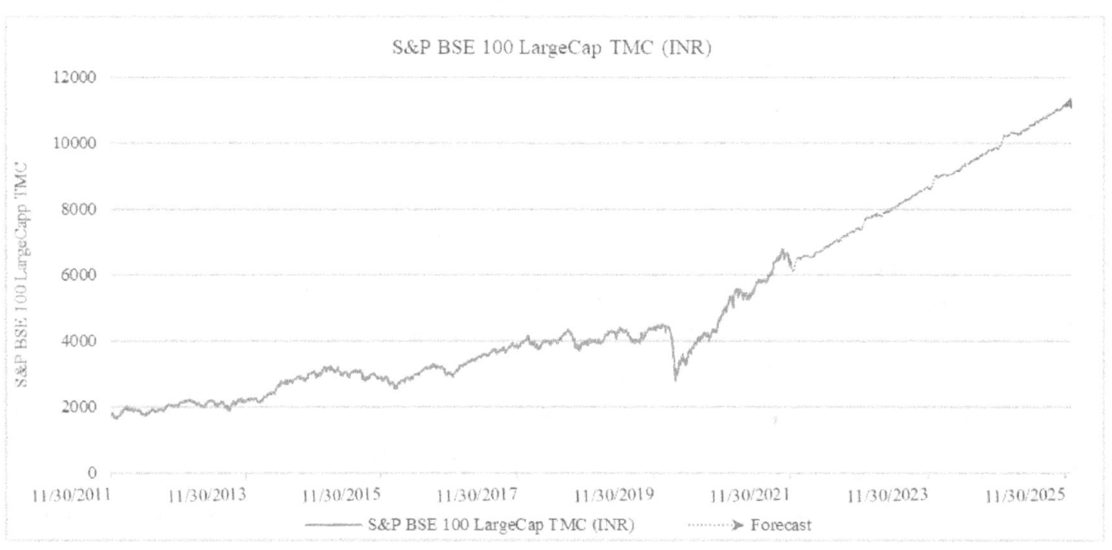

Calculation of pension- OPS:

In this calculation, if the employee retires as per the old pension regime, then the amount (at the time of settlement) is calculated on the basis of the prevailing interest rate in the calculation of GPF. In this calculation, the rate of interest on GPF each year has been deducted at the rate of 0.1% in the following years, according to the previous trends with an assumption of minimum 6% interest.

Without Commutation				
Basic	Pension	D.A. %	D.A.	Total Pension
22,78,300	11,39,150	48%	5,46,792	16,85,942
Total				16,85,942

Total Benefits at the time of Retirement under Old Pension

Total Benefit for Retirement		
1	Gratuity	3,75,91,950
2	Commutation	4,55,66,000
3	Pension	16,85,942
4	GPF Claim	6,95,19,744
5	Leave Encashment	3,47,31,160
Total Retirement Benefit		18,90,94,796

Interest on GPF amount @ rate of 6% (not including pension amount)

Interest on GPF account for pensioners			
S.NO.	Claim	Yearly Interest	Monthly Interest
1	18,74,08,853	9,37,044	78,087

He will also receive a pension of Rs.16,85,942/- per month and monthly interest of Rs.78,087/-, if he deposits total retirement benefit in bank account.

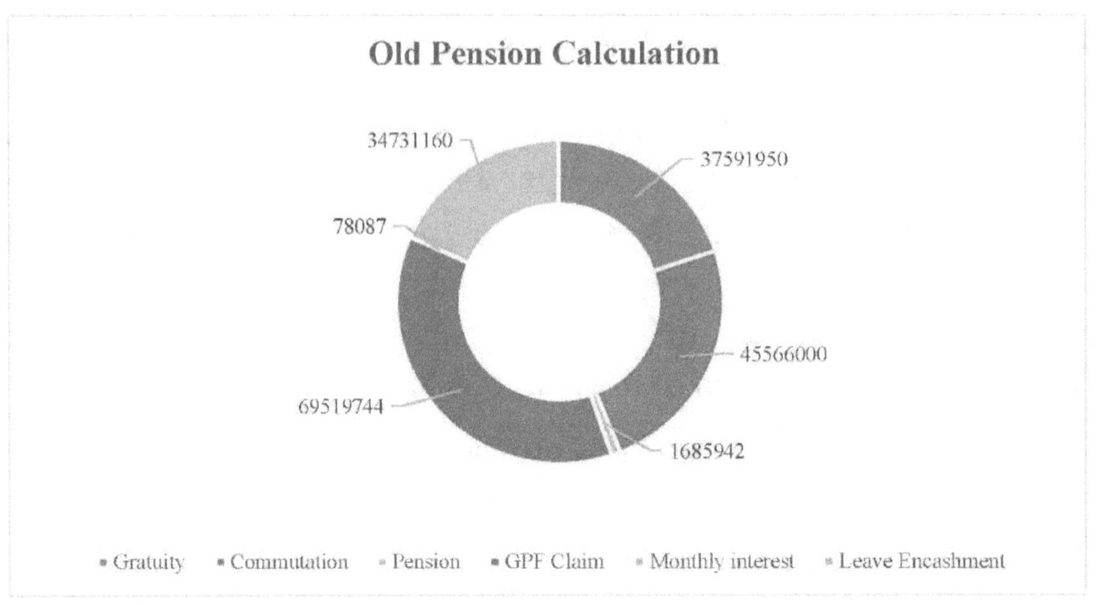

Calculation of pension NPS:

- If the employee has been appointed to the State Service on or after January 2016, the estimated return was based on 10 years' return which is 9.85 per annum.

- The pension calculation in the National Pension System has been done on the basis of 750/- per lakh per month.

Without Commutation					
S.NO.	Claim Amount	60% Cash	40% For Pension	Pension @ 750/ Per Lack	Total Pension
1	290948272	174568963	116379309	872845	872845
Total					872845

Total Benefit for Retirement under New Pension

	Total Benefit for Retirement	
1	Gratuity	37591950
2	Commutation	45566000
3	Pension	872845
4	NPS Claim	174568963
5	Leave Encashment	34731160
	Total Retirement Benefit	**293330918**

Interest on NPS amount @ rate of 6% (not including pension amount)

	Interest on GPF account for pensioners		
S.NO.	Claim	Yearly Interest	Monthly Interest
1	292458073	1462290	121858

He will also receive a pension of Rs. 8,72,845/- per month and monthly interest of Rs.1,21,858/- if he deposits total retirement benefit in the bank account.

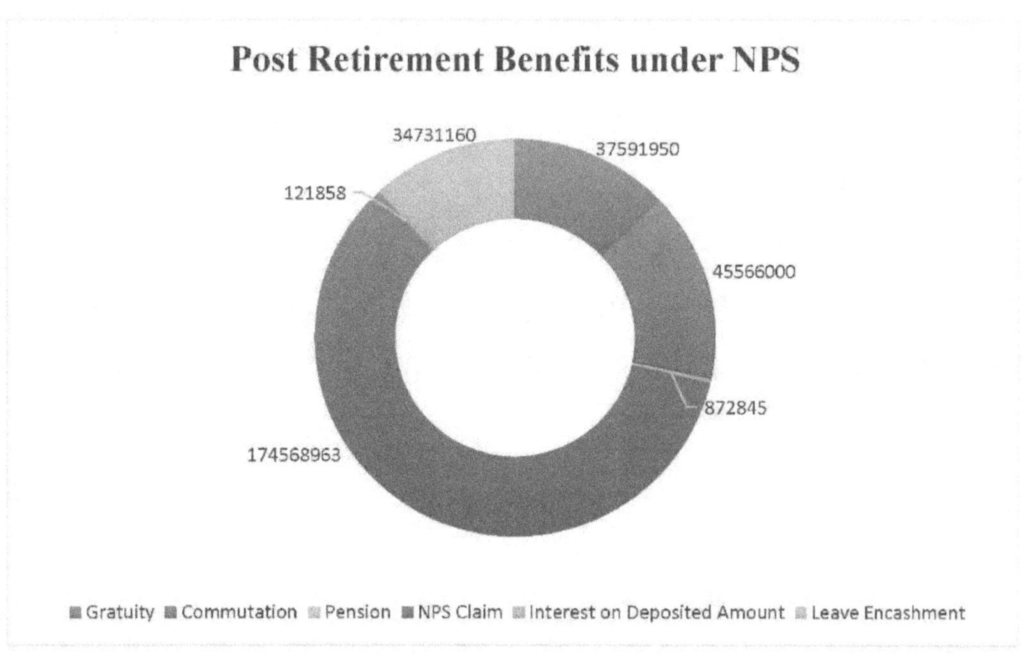

Comparison between OPS and NPS:

In the long run, the contribution to NPS will create a corpus and can earn better returns with the benefit of tax deduction on withdrawal of corpus.

On the day of superannuation, an employee will get the following emoluments:

Category	OPS	NPS
Gratuity	3,75,91,950	3,75,91,950
Commutation	4,55,66,000	4,55,66,000
Pension	16,85,942	8,72,845
GPF Claim	6,95,19,744	-----
60 % of the total accumulated corpus	-----	17,45,68,963
Monthly Interest @ 6%	78,087	1,21,858
Leave Encashment	3,47,31,160	3,47,31,160
Total Fund on retirement	**18,91,72,883**	**29,34,52,776**

Similar amount received by OPS and NPS employees on superannuation

(Gratuity, Commutation and Leave Encashment)

As per the calculation above, Gratuity amount, Commutation and Leave Encashment amount are the same in both the pension schemes.

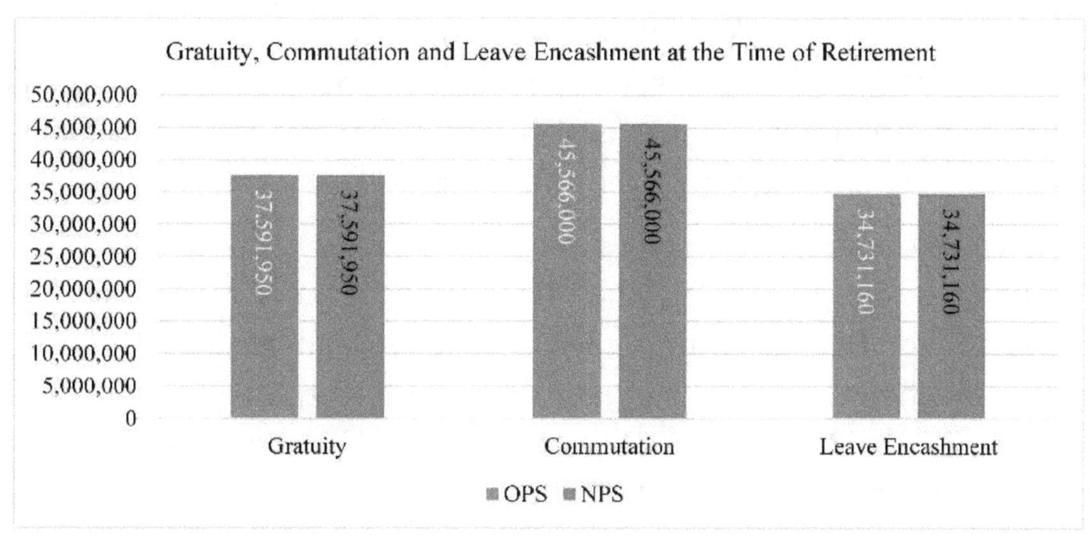

Different amount received by OPS and NPS employees

(GPF claims, withdrawal of corpus, interest and monthly pension)

On the superannuation, employee gets 60 percent of total corpus amount to Rs. 17,45,68,963 whereas in OPS, employee gets final GPF claim amounts to Rs. 6,95,19,744.

Scheme	Final Claim	Interest	Monthly Pension
NPS	17,45,68,963	1,21,858	8,72,845
OPS	6,95,19,744	78,087	16,85,942

As per above tables, total emoluments received by a NPS employee is significantly higher than an OPS employee. Amount received in gratuity, commutation and leave encashment are same for the both schemes. The different amounts received by the employees are final claim, interest and pension. In the pension head, the OPS employee gets almost double the monthly pension from the NPS employee. In the interest head, the NPS employee gets higher monthly interest than the OPS employee. As a final claim, OPS employees get GPF amount whereas NPS employees get 60 percent withdrawal from total corpus, which is 2.5 times higher compared to OPS final claim. It is also relevant to mention here that the rest of the 40 percent corpus is deposited to annuity service providers (ASPs) for pension, this amount is also received by the spouse or family member as per plan chosen by the employee.

If the complete amount received on superannuation is deposited into GPF account for pensioners, the NPS employee gets higher interest compared to OPS employee. The monthly amount receivable to employees after retirement are pension and interest, the OPS employee gets Rs. 17,64,029 per month whereas the NPS employee gets Rs. 9,94,703 per month. It is clear from the above discussion that in the case of the total amount received on superannuation, the NPS employee is on the upper hand as he received almost 1.5 times higher compared to the OPS employee. With this amount, he can plan to purchase immovable property or deposit it into a bank etc. On the other hand, the monthly pension which is crucial for recurring and household expenses, OPS is far better than an NPS employee.

Final settlement amount in OPS and NPS

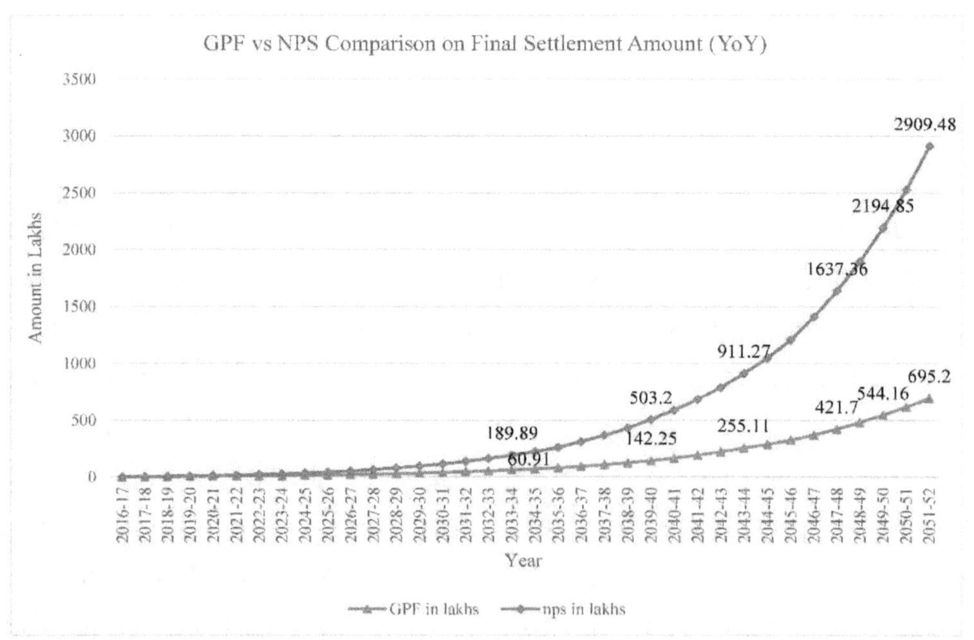

Comparative analysis of benefits under National pension schemes and Old pension systems for Government employees

Sn	Component	National pension schemes (NPS)	Old pension systems (OPS)
1	Contribution	Employee's contribution of 10 % and Govt. contribution of 10%, of employee salary	Pension if backed by the Government
2	Commencement of Pension	After attaining 60 years of age, 40% of the amount of consolidated contribution in NPS is purchased with annuity at market rate, the amount generated will be considered as pension.	Pension is started soon after the next month of retirement.
3	Pension Commutation	Under NPS 60% amount is paid to the contributor on attaining age of 60 years and said amount is exempted from tax.	One third of the amount of pension can be taken in advance for many years which is exempted from tax. It is an alternative system.
4	D.A.	Only a fixed pension is given in the chosen plan. No effect of DA is on annuity-based pension	D.A. gets increased every 6 months. As a result of which an increased DA amount is added to the basic pension amount.
5	Monthly Pension Amount	Depends on annuity plan under NPS contributor has option to choose type of annuity and annuity service provides based or above principles these are your types of options are available as following- (1) Annuity for life (2) Annuity for life with return of purchase price on death (3) Annuity payable for life	Pension is given after 28 years of service with a fixed pension of 50% of last drawn salary at the time of retirement. If service is less than 28 years but more than 10 years then pension is based on proportionate method.

Sn	Component	National pension schemes (NPS)	Old pension systems (OPS)
		with 100 percent annuity payable to spouse on death of annuitant. (4) Annuity for life with a provision for 100 per cent of the annuity payable to the spouse for the annuitant for life on death of the annuitant, with return of purchase price on the death of last survivor.	
6	Gratuity	Salary of 16.5 months or as per the recommendation of 7th Pay Commission an amount of 20 lacs rupees which is exempted from tax.	Salary of 16.5 months or as per the recommendation of 7th Pay Commission an amount of 20 lacs rupees which is exempted from tax.
7	VRS	Out of total consolidated contribution of employee 80% of the amount of annuity is purchased and the remaining 20% is given directly to employee.	After 23 year of service all benefits of pension are given in VRS.
8	Pension Provider	Regulator of NPS is PFRDA with the help of NSDL and NPS trust.	Pension is provided by the pension department of Government.
9	Death Gratuity	In case of demise during service tenure, 33 months of salary or as per recommendation of 7th pay commission 20 lacs rupees is given.	In case of demise during service tenure, 33 months of salary or as per recommendation of 7th pay commission 20 lacs rupees is given.
10	Pension in case of death during service	Under NPS or demise during service hence minimum 80% of total consolidated pension amount is given to person nominated by subscriber or to legal heir as annuity pension and remaining 20% is given as one time amount is given to	Along with death gratuity and other benefits full pensions are given to spouses for 10 year or in case spouse is not alive then family pension is given to adult children.

Sn	Component	National pension schemes (NPS)	Old pension systems (OPS)
		person nominated by subscriber or legal heir but if at the time of death of subscriber consolidated amount is 2 lacs or less then entire amount is given to person nominated by subscriber or legal heir without annuity. There is provision of additional help in form of family pension by Government.	
11	Eligibility of pension	Annuity depends on contribution of pension and pension is given on completion of 60 years of age and there is no minimum service hence is required.	After 10 year of service tenure complete benefits of old pension (after 01-1-2006) but minimum service hence is required.
12	Minimum pension	Assessment of pension is based mainly on an annuity	Minimum pension of 3500 Rupees
13	Additional benefits	Based on the annuity plan	Additional benefits to the family pensioner/basic pension the o pensioner is given as follows: - Age limit 80 to 84 years 20% 85 to 89 years 30% 90 to 94 years 40% 95 to 99 years 50% 100 years or above 100%

Recommendation for the betterment of NPS, following changes in NPS architecture is required-

1. Death during the service-

This is a crucial period for an employee's family to have to tackle the financial situation without the employee. Government should not leave behind the family only on annuity-based pension. It is also necessary on the grounds of social security. In this area benefits must be the same as the old pension system. Pension to the spouse for 10 years or in case the spouse is not alive, then family pension be given to adult children. Pension should not be less than 33 percent of the last drawn salary. If the spouse gets an annuity-based pension less than 33 percent of the last drawn salary then the difference amount should be borne by the Government.

2. Effect of Dearness allowance and pay commission

    (i)   Employees under the old pension system will get the benefit of DA on their salary but in NPS scheme there is no effect of DA on employees' annuity-based pension. By a logical effect, the Government should contribute 10 percent of the increased DA into the employee's annuity fund.

    (ii)   Employees under the old pension system will get the benefit of pay commission on their pension but under NPS, pensioners aren't getting any benefit of the pay revision. In the same thread, a DA pensioner under NPS should also get the benefit of paying commission revisions.

3. Rules and regulations are framed in such a way that the employee can choose the best fit plan for his own will, and the regulator should prepare various plans for different kinds of

employees based on their risk-taking capacities, pay scale and other parameters.

4. Once employees switch job from center to state government or private job to government, PRAN number should not change. NSDL has facilities in their module but DDOs are not using this module. If DDOs adopt this module then the issue related to tracing of legacy amounts and their uploading is solved.

5. Employee should get a monthly detailed statement of transition (SoT) in which he will get monthly return on every sector of his investments i.e. G-Sec, debt fund, asset backed investment, equity and related investment (also detailed transition of large cap fund to small cap fund).

6. Compulsory PRAN generation Module- There is online PRAN generation module (OPGM) available at CRA-NSDL but in many state governments physical PRAN generations were done on the basis of submission of physical form and this whole process took 10 to 15 days. However, using the OPGM facility, the PRAN is issued within 3 days which results in speedy work and also reduces the fees up to Rs10 per PRAN.

7. Subscriber Contribution File (SCF) generation through Portal-the monthly subscription (SC+GC) is uploaded on CRA-NSDL portal. Presently, in many state governments, the contribution of the government and the employee are manually matched to the data and then uploaded on the NSDL portal. This whole process takes a month or so which results in delay in the uploading of the contribution amount. It also hinders the accumulated fund of the subscriber as the Net Asset Value (NAV) on the accumulated fund is also delayed. If the whole process is done online than subscribers of the NPS scheme will be incalculably benefited as

they will receive the Net Asset Value for the current month 20 days before. The accumulated fund of the subscriber will be immeasurably increased and will be in the best interest of the subscriber.

8. The regulation and rules of PFRDA should be compulsory for the state government so that employees' interests can be secured. PFRDA has given the choice to the employee to choose any one of the private pension funds but few state governments have adopted instruction. In the other case, PFRDA has issued a notification regarding a hike in government contribution, but no state government has adopted this notification. Only the central government has opted for this notification. The state government should also adopt all the circulars and notifications issued by the PFRDA in toto as the central government adopted.

Conclusion

Government employees have budgetary planning for every small and big events of their family requirement. Their planning includes predictable present to prospects salary and also the amount they received as emoluments after retirement including pension. In the condition of predictable future prospects, psychologies of Government employees are also biased toward certainty and security. In this scenario most of the government employees consider the OPS better because it gives them certainty, security sustainability, adequacy and confidence. The certainty and other parameters are so high that employees do not want to compare rate of return or other benefits of NPS. Their only demand is to get pension at fixed equal to 50 per cent of his last drawn salary. In contrast, NPS is a Definitive Contribution Pension Scheme, that is, the pension amount depends on the number of years the job has been done and the annuity amount. The benefits of NPS are not popularized as it should be, that is why employees are not much aware of merits and demerits of NPS compared to the well established OPS.

References:

- www.sipf.rajasthan.gov.in
- www.ri.org.in
- www.pfrda.org.in
- www.npstrust.org.in
- www.cransdl.orgin
- www.moneycontrol.com

Decadal Review of NPS in Rajasthan

Contents

Decadal review of NPS in Rajasthan

Introduction

National Pension System (NPS) is a defined contributory pension system in which contributions from the government employee along with matching contributions from government as an employer, are collected by Government's nodal agency and transferred to an employee's PRAN, maintained NSDL-CRA, a Central Record keeping Agency (CRA) and designated Pension Funds (PFs), as may be specified by regulations. As per the guidelines, it is mandatory for every employee to contribute 10 percent of basic pay and dearness allowance every month from salary and equal, or as prescribed by government, contribution is to be made by the State Government. The contribution details and corresponding amounts and complete NPS architecture are regulated and managed by Pension Fund Regulatory & Development Authority (PFRDA), the National Securities Depository Limited (NSDL) and NPS trust. The NPS works under an umbrella architecture with each function assigned to a separate institution. The NPS architecture consists of Points of Presence (POP), Government Department Nodal Offices, Central Record-keeping Agency (CRA), Trustee Bank, Pension Fund Managers (PFM's), NPS Trust, Custodian, Annuity Service Providers and Retirement Advisers.

NPS is mandatory to all employees joining services of Central Government (except Armed Forces) and Central Autonomous Bodies on or after 1st January 2004. Government of Rajasthan adopted NPS architecture and has implemented NPS mandatorily through Gazette

Notifications for the State Government/ Autonomous body employees joining on or after 01.01.2004.

Tax Benefits for NPS

1. On Employee's contribution: Employee's own contribution is eligible for tax deduction under sec 80 CCD (1) of Income Tax Act up to 10% of salary (Basic + DA). This is within the overall ceiling of Rs. 1.50 Lacs under Sec. 80 CCE of the Income Tax Act.

2. On Employer's contribution: Up to 10% of Basic & DA (no monetary ceiling) under 80CCD (2). This rebate is over and above 80 CCE limits of Rs 1.50 lacs.

3. From F.Y. 2015-16, a subscriber has been allowed tax deduction in addition to the deduction allowed under Sec. 80CCD (1) for contribution in his NPS account subject to a maximum of Rs 50,000/- under Sec. 80CCD 1(B). At present, at the time of exit, the amount utilized for the purchase of annuity is tax exempted. From 1st April 2016, 40% of the total accumulated corpus under NPS has

been made tax free. Further, from FY 2017-18 onwards, partial withdrawals will be treated as tax free.

A Facilities to NPS Subscribers: Central Record-keeping agency provides following set of IT and system enabled services to the subscriber

a. SMS alerts on: Subscriber registration, Credit/Debit of units in the subscriber account, Fund value in subscriber's account (quarterly alert), Withdrawal.

b. Email alerts on: Subscriber registration, Credit/Debit of units in the subscriber account, change in subscriber details, nomination details and any other activity related to subscriber details, Grievance log & Resolution and Withdrawal.

c. Centralized Grievance Management System (CGMS) with a pre-determined turnaround time for resolution of grievances related to different services.

d. Periodic consolidated SOT (Statement of Transactions).

e. Subscriber awareness programmes at various locations and centers.

f. Subscriber can update his/her mobile no. & email id by logging into the CRA system through his I-Pin

g. Subscriber can change his/her I-Pin through OTP process.

h. NPS Mobile App Investments of NPS Contributions: Your contributions are routed to pension funds for investments across different asset classes, as per the investment guidelines prescribed by the authority from time to time.

To the extent of exposure in the National Pension System, in different categories of investments including Government securities, debt securities and equity as per PFRDA rules. For investment in different categories of investments PFRDA appointed and registered pension funds to manage the NPS corpus. Pension funds follow investment guidelines, exposure limits as per PFRDA's rules. There are seven authorized pension funds for investing in the NPS corpus namely

(i) HDFC Pension Management Co. Ltd. (ii) ICICI Prudential Pension Fund Management Co. Ltd. (iii) Kotak Mahindra Pension Fund Ltd. (iv) LIC Pension Fund Ltd. (v) SBI Pension Funds Pvt. Ltd (vi) UTI Retirement Solutions Pvt. Ltd (vii) Birla Sun Life Pension Management Limited.

At present, central and state government NPS funds are being allocated to three Pension Funds (PFS) viz SBI Pension Funds Private Limited, UTI Retirement Solutions Limited, and LIC Pension Fund Limited which are being invested by each pension fund as per investment guidelines issued by PFRDA.

As per PFRDA rules corpus of central and state government sector maximum exposure limits are following (i) Government Securities & related investments 55 percent (ii) Debt Instruments & Related investments 45 percent (iii) Asset-backed, trust structured & Miscellaneous investments 5 percent (iv) Short term debt instruments & related investments 10 percent (v) Equity & related investments 15 percent.

Further, from 2019 Government subscribers are free to choose any one of the pension funds including private sector pension funds. They could change their option once a year. From 2019, Government employees will also have the freedom to choose the investment pattern given by PFRDA. Following are the investment pattern (i) Existing scheme in which funds are allocated by the PFRDA among three Public Sector Undertaking fund managers based on their past performance in accordance with the guidelines of PFRDA for

Government employees shall continue as the fault scheme for both existing and new subscribers. (ii) Government employees who prefer a fixed return with a minimum amount of risk shall be given an option to invest 100% of the funds in Government securities (Scheme G) (iii) Government employees who prefer higher returns shall be given the options of the following two life-cycle based schemes: (a) Conservative life cycle fund with maximum exposure to equity capped at 25% - LC-25 (b) Moderate life cycle fund with maximum exposure to equity capped at 50% - LC-50. The Government subscribers under NPS may choose one of the above investments.

NPS in Rajasthan

NPS was made applicable to the employees appointed on or after 01-01-2004 in Government State Autonomous Bodies (SAB) vide the Rajasthan Government circular dated 12-08-2004. To implement NPS architecture, various notifications were issued by the Government of Rajasthan. Memorandum dated 27.03.2004 and Rajasthan Civil services (Contributory Pension) Rules, 2005 were issued for Government employees are few of them.

To implement an effective regulatory framework of NPS Scheme in Rajasthan, PFRDA Architecture was adopted in Toto wide FD (Rules Division) order dated 27.08.2009 and administrative control was given to State Insurance and Provident Fund for NPS in Rajasthan. Further, to create an effective regulatory framework, agreements were signed with NSDL and NPS Trust on 09.11.2010 and 02.12.2010 respectively.

Rajasthan government employees' under National Pension System (NPS)

In the state government around eight lakh employees are working out of which more than 60 percent of employees are under NPS and the rest of the employees are under the old pension system. In the year 2011, only 15 percent of total state government employees were covered under NPS.

The number of Rajasthan government employees' subscribers under the National Pension System (NPS) rose from 1.13 lakh in 2011 to 4.89 lakh in 2020, showing a year-on-year (Y-o-Y) impressive growth. Percentage share of NPS employees under cumulative of all State Governments, Rajasthan has consistent between 7 to 9 percent. From the table, it is also inferred that from 2017 to 2021, year on year growth of NPS the subscription of the Rajasthan Government was much higher than other state governments. It means that during this time employment generation by the Rajasthan government was much higher than other state governments.

Other states	Rajasthan	FY	Rajasthan share in all state government Subscribers	Other	Rajasthan	All India	FY	Number of Subscribers under NPS and Cumulative YoY NPS Subscribers Status
91%	9%	2011-2012		1144393	117889	1262282	**2011-2012**	
92%	8%	2012-2013		1626224	139328	1765552	**2012-2013**	
92%	8%	2013-2014		1991455	162128	2153583	**2013-2014**	
93%	7%	2014-2015		2630194	200868	2831062	**2014-2015**	
93%	7%	2015-2016		2923882	223259	3147141	**2015-2016**	
93%	7%	2016-2017		3332526	266895	3599421	**2016-2017**	
91%	9%	2017-2018		3868000	361501	4229501	**2017-2018**	
91%	9%	2018-2019		4321325	430502	4751827	**2018-2019**	
91%	9%	2019-2020		4754000	455298	5209298	**2019-2020**	
91%	9%	2020-2021		4897000	496944	5393944	**2020-2021**	

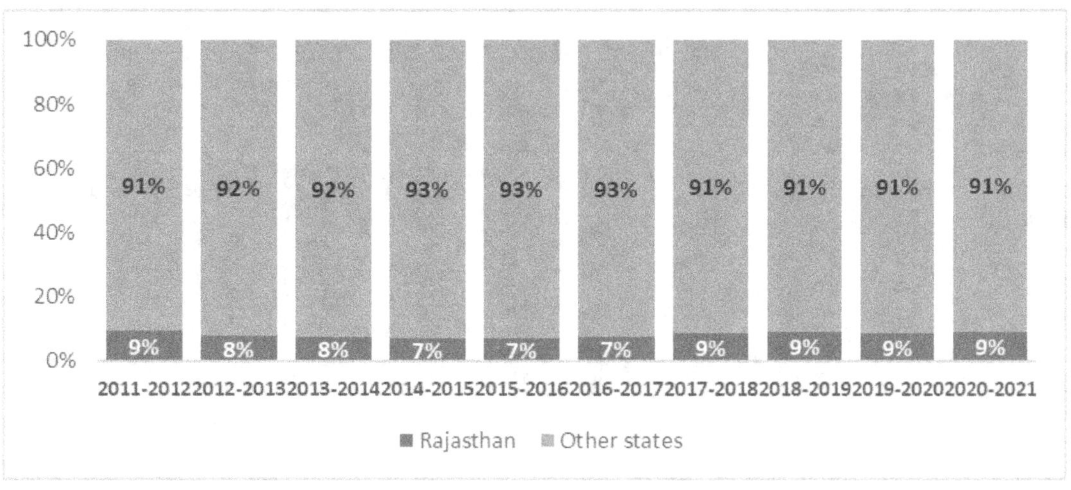

Assets under management (AUM)

Assets under management are the overall market value of corpus invested by NPS holders. NPS Corpus invested by the state government employees' assets under management rose from 101 crore in 2011 to 16350 crore in 2019. Percentage share of assets under management cumulative of all state governments, Rajasthan has consistent stayed between 7 to 9 per cent.

Total Assets under Management under NPS Cumulative YoY AUM Status (in Cr)									
FY	2011-2012	2012-2013	2013-2014	2014-2015	2015-2016	2016-2017	2017-2018	2018-2019	2019-2020
Other states	3420	10489	20211	36244	57693	84917	115679	158491	211023
Rajasthan	101	1283	2532	3916	5624	7742	10290	14410	16350
All India	3521	11772	22743	40160	63317	92659	125969	172901	227373
Rajasthan share in all state government AUM									
FY	2011-2012	2012-2013	2013-2014	2014-2015	2015-2016	2016-2017	2017-2018	2018-2019	2019-2020
Rajasthan	2.87	10.90	11.13	9.75	8.88	8.36	8.17	8.33	7.19
Other states	97.13	89.10	88.87	90.25	91.12	91.64	91.83	91.67	92.81

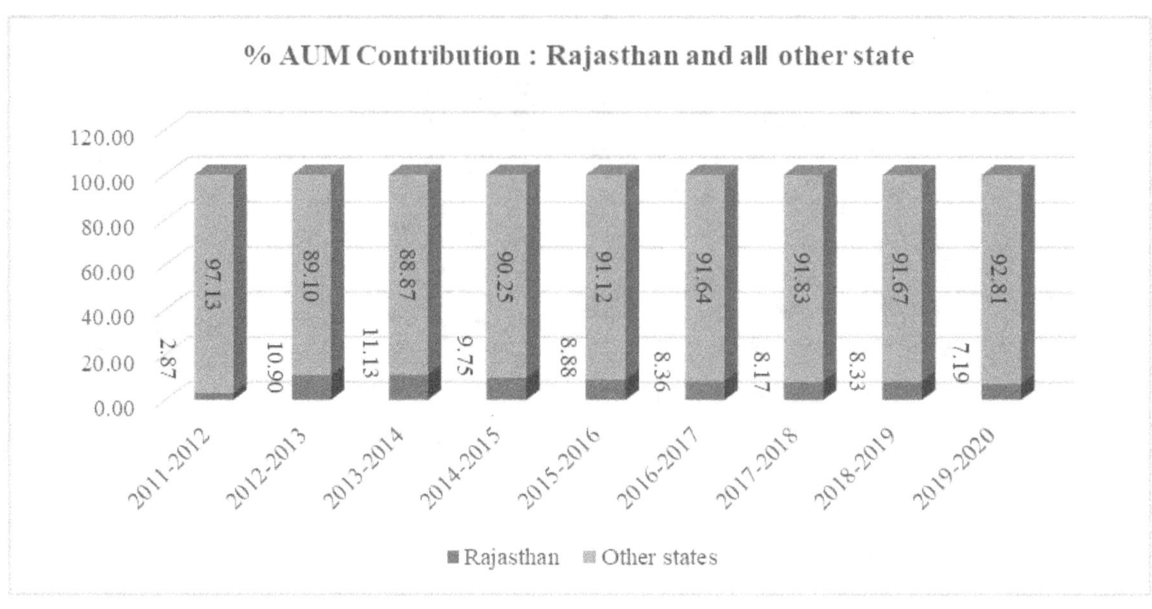

Legacy amount transferred to the NSDL

The contribution details and corresponding Government amounts are being transferred to the NSDL since November 2011. Prior to November 2011, the employee contribution was regularly deposited into pension accounts and employer contributions were being deposited in the state Government PD account. The amount deposited before 2011, termed as legacy amount, which had to be transferred to NSDL amounting to ₹ 1394 crore (employees contribution, employee co-contribution and corresponding interest) was lying with the state Government at the end of 2011.

The detail of legacy amount transferred to the NSDL is given in the table below:

Details of legacy Amount

(₹ in crore)

Balance Legacy as on	Total Legacy Amount in Opening Balance	Total Uploaded Amount During the Year	Balance Legacy Amount	Interest	Net Balance of Legacy Amount
1	2	3	4	5	6
Upto 31.10.2011	1394	0	1394	0	1394
01.11.2011 to 31.03.2012	1394	0	1394	97	1491
2012-13	1491	613	878	56	934
2013-14	934	364	570	60	630
2014-15	630	297	333	37	370
2015-16	369	131	238	35	273
2016-17	273	161	112	9	121
2017-18	120	65	55	7	62
2018-19	63	20	43	4	47
2019-20	46	10	36	7	43
2020-21	44	7	37	1	38

From the above table, it is evident that as on 31st March 2019, balance amount of ₹46.43 crore on account of legacy amount is pending for transfer.

Total legacy amount in opening balance to total uploaded amount during the year, year on year bases, from 2011 to 2012 no legacy uploadation work was done. From 2013 to 2017 legacy uploadation work was done on priority basis. Better uploadation was done because the state government had segregated employees whose ledger entries were properly maintained. If employees' ledger is properly maintained then the monthly contribution has to be calculated and matching government contribution deposited to NSDL. Once the properly maintained ledger amount is uploaded, the state government picks up employees whose ledger was traceable and how it was maintained.

Once these entries were uploaded, the further identification of legacy entries were difficult for certain reasons like multiple employee ID, frequent transfers, offices closed and transfer record to other DDO offices, transfer of DDO office, merger of offices and employees switch services. Now calculation of legacy amount is a difficult task that is why after 2017, progress of legacy amount uploadation work was slower. Another biggest area of problem was panchyati raj institution (PRI) and state autonomous bodies (SAB) where employee's data maintenance and integration was poor, so a lot of legacy amount belongs to them.

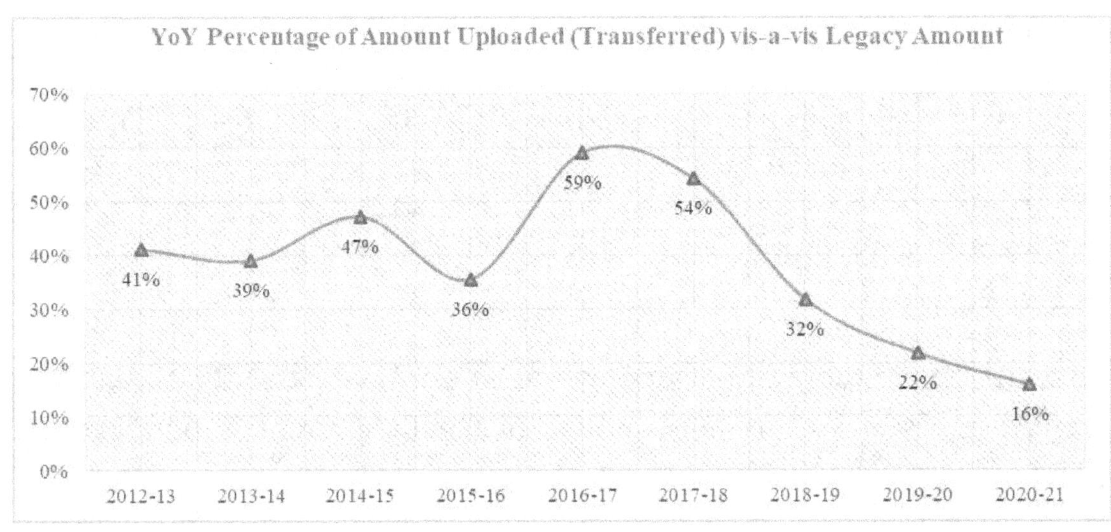

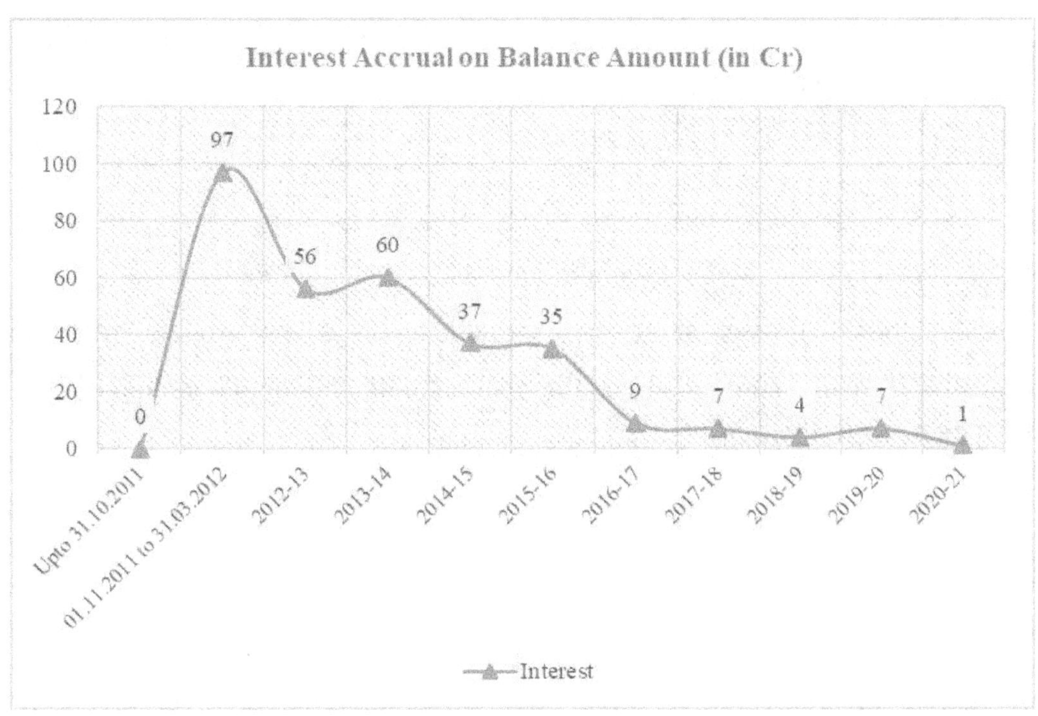

NPS Contribution and uploadation of State Government Employees

The details of transfer of NPS of both state government and all India services officer's employees and employer's contribution to NSDL/trustee bank as on march end every year.

Table: Contribution of State Government Employees

(₹ in crore)

Period	Opening Balances	Employees Contribution	Employees Contribution	Total (2+3+4)	Upload Employees Contribution	Upload Employer Contribution	Total Upload Amount (6+7)	% Upload (5/8)	Remaining Employees Contribution (5-8)
1	2	3	4	5	6	7	8	9	10
2011-12	0	198	0	198	51	51	102	51	96
2012-13	96	204	158	459	206	206	412	89	47
2013-14	47	247	206	500	206	206	412	82	88
2014-15	88	363	355	806	355	355	710	88	96
2015-16	96	501	516	1113	517	517	1034	92	79

2016-17	79	681	698	1458	698	698	1396	95	62
2017-18	62	1156	1082	2300	1082	1082	2164	92	136
2018-19	136	1765	1797	3698	1797	1797	3594	97	104
2019-20	104	2187	2187	4478					
2020-21	0	2440	2440	4880					
Total	708	9742	9439	19890	4912	4912	9824		708

The chart above shows that uploadation of government matching contribution was marginally on the lower side as compared to employees' contribution.

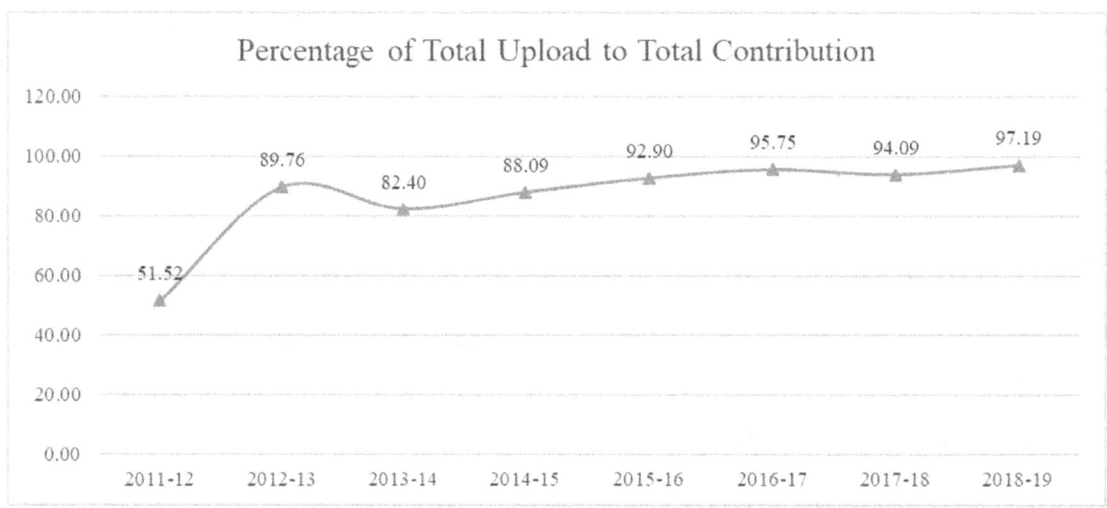

Except in the initial year 2011, average percentage of total uploadation to total contribution is hovering around 90 to 95 per cent.

Expected withdrawal to reported withdrawal under NPS- summary

Sector	No of Superannuation / attainment of 60 years cases for the year as per CRA Database	No. of Actual Superannuation/ 60 yrs. cases reported as on the last date of the year
Rajasthan	3,297	2,180
2011-2012	75	-
2012-2013	244	1
2013-2014	332	14
2014-2015	365	475
2015-2016	374	418
2016-2017	381	383
2017-2018	455	354
2018-2019	485	269
2019-2020	586	266
Other State Governments	47,629	24,992
2011-2012	475	-
2012-2013	1,538	10
2013-2014	2,887	158
2014-2015	3,965	1,555
2015-2016	4,910	2,621
2016-2017	6,388	4,705
2017-2018	7,108	5,435
2018-2019	8,443	5,844
2019-2020	11,915	4,664
FY	% Of expected to actual superannuation (Rajasthan)	% Of expected to actual superannuation (Other States)
2011-2012	-	-
2012-2013	0	1
2013-2014	4	5
2014-2015	130	47
2015-2016	112	58
2016-2017	101	75
2017-2018	78	77
2018-2019	55	68
2019-2020	45	39

The above table shows that as per the database of NSDL how many government employees attain superannuation. This means NSDL get withdrawal request from employees through state nodal agencies. The share of Rajasthan, cumulative of all state government employees who attain superannuation, gradually moved downward from 15.78 percent to 4.9 percent.

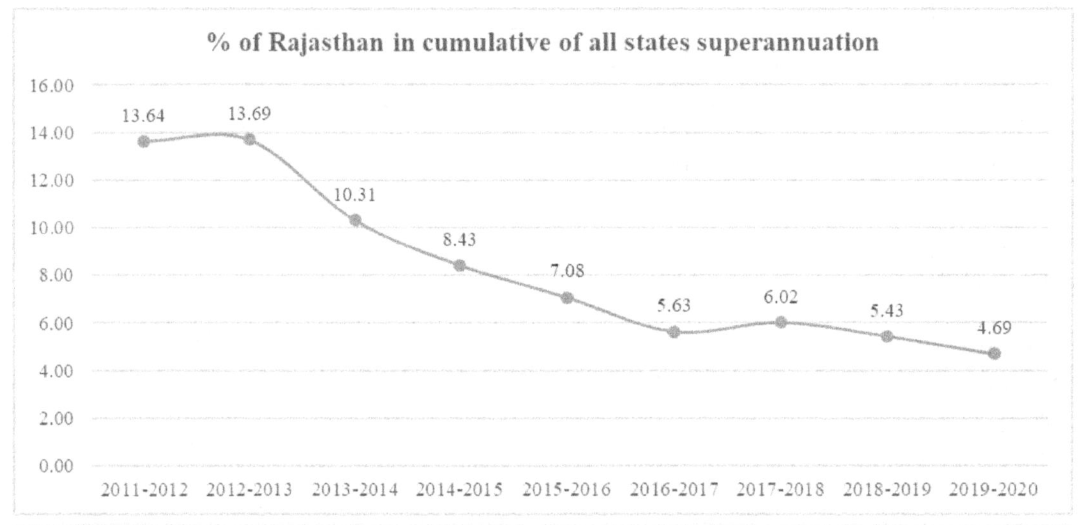

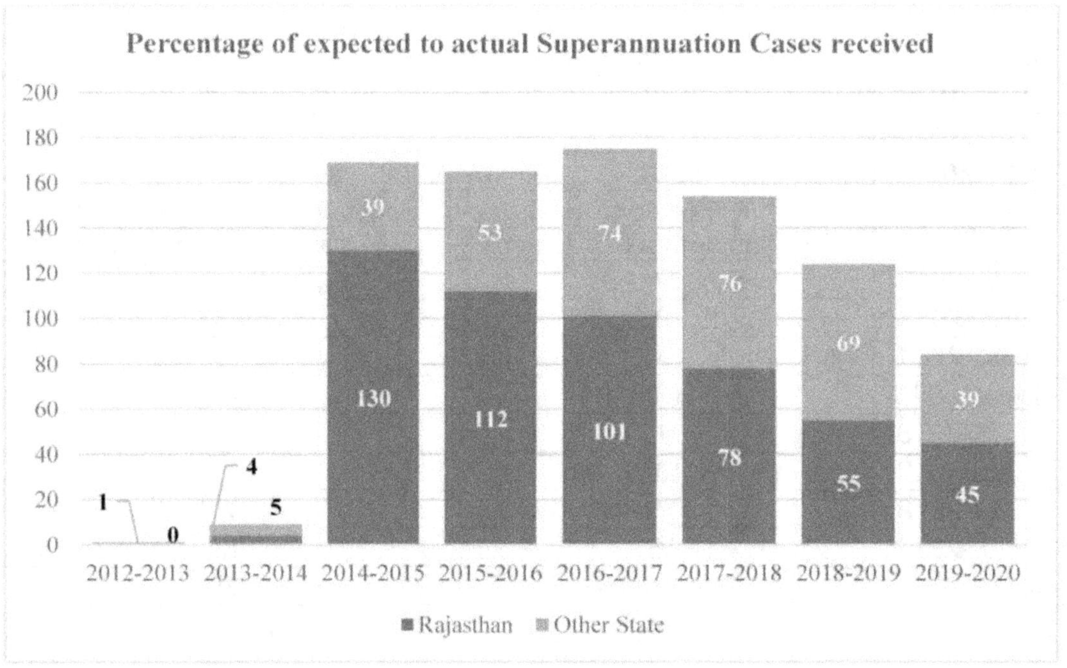

From the table shown above, it is clear that retired employees did not complete the process related to withdrawal at the time of retirement or even submitted the withdrawal request, and there were some shortcomings in the withdrawal form or the state nodal agency did not forward it to NSDL. From the year 2011 to 2013, no work related to withdrawal was done. If we see the cumulative progress from 2011 to 2019, 52 percent of employees withdrawal request has been finalized in other states, while Rajasthan's situation is a bit fine, here the withdrawal request of 66 percent of retired employees has been finalized.

DDOs are regularly sensitized employees who are going to retire in near future. Withdrawal requests have not been received from employees due to ignorance and lack of clarity of rules among the employees, even DDOs. State Nodal Agency (SIPF) held periodical meetings, training programs to process claim cases from employees. CRA also sent emails, SMS, and letters to employees for the withdrawal process.

Analysis of withdrawal request received to request a processed and total amount of withdrawals.

Annual Withdrawal Summary as on 2019

Level	Withdrawal type	Request Received to Request Processed
Rajasthan	Death	99.15
Rajasthan	Pre-Mature Exit	97.27
Rajasthan	Superannuation	97.54
Other State Governments	Death	94.52
Other State Governments	Pre-Mature Exit	95.13
Other State Governments	Superannuation	97.11

There are three categories of withdrawal namely death, premature exit, and superannuation. As withdrawal summary up to 2019, request received (online and physical) to final request, the final settled performance of Rajasthan is better than rest of Indian states in all the three categories.

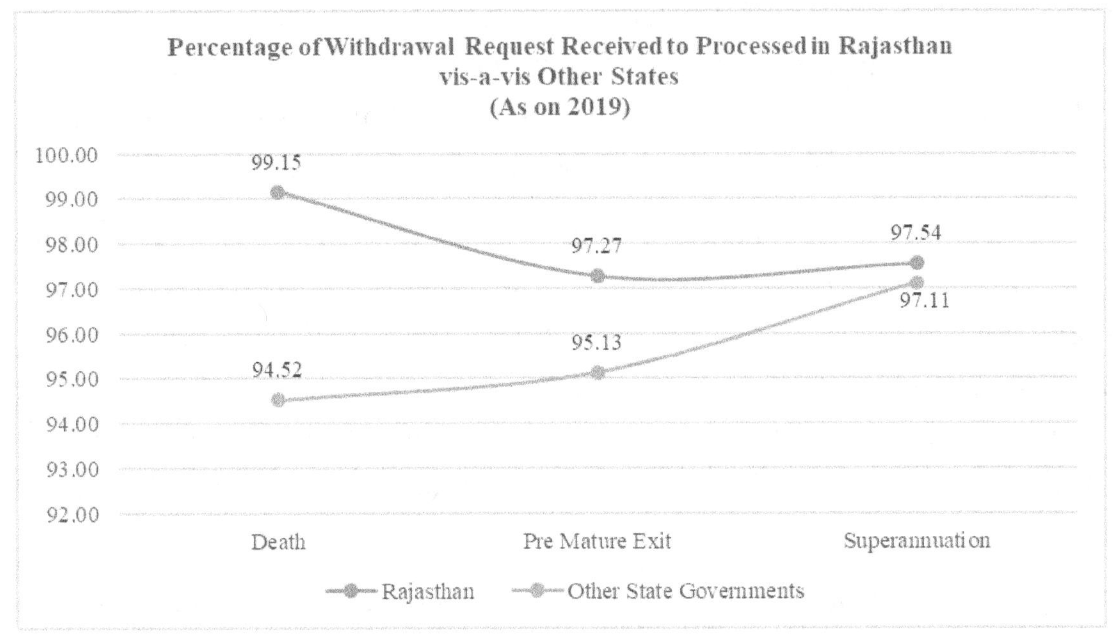

Status of Online Withdrawal Requests Received		
Withdrawal Type	Rajasthan	Other States
Death	66%	87%
Pre-Mature Exit	67%	84%
Superannuation	56%	80%

According to withdrawal summary up to 2019, although withdrawal request received and request processed performance of Rajasthan is better than rest of India, online withdrawal request submission to total request received of Rajasthan is far behind.

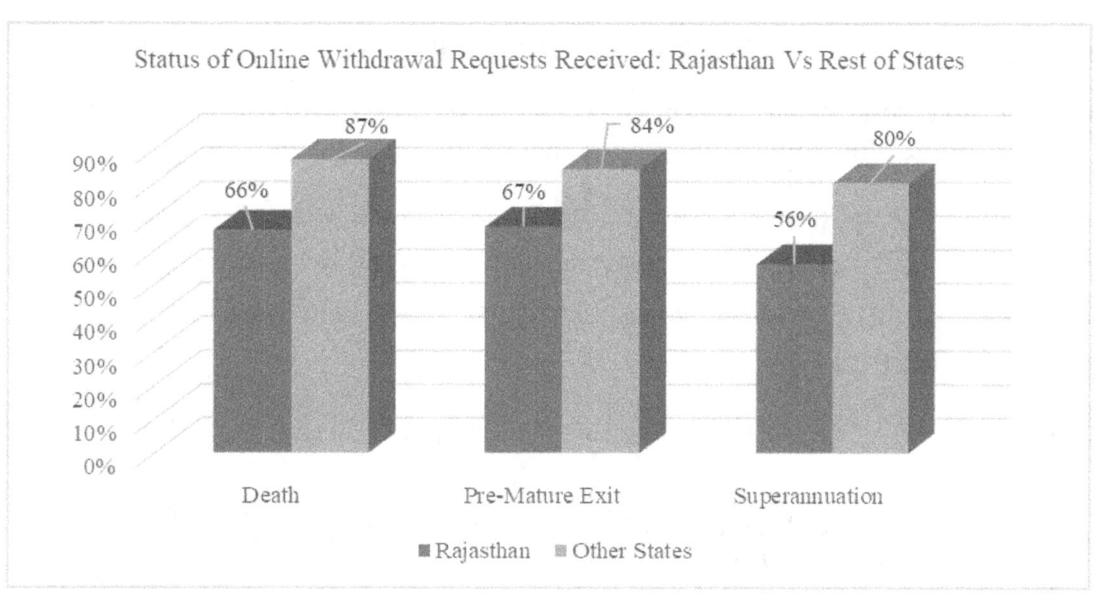

Withdrawal amounts on per case-exit

In lakh

Region	Death	Pre-Mature Exit	Superannuation
Rajasthan	3.38	4.09	5.78
Other States	2.63	2.58	3.69
All India	2.73	2.65	3.86

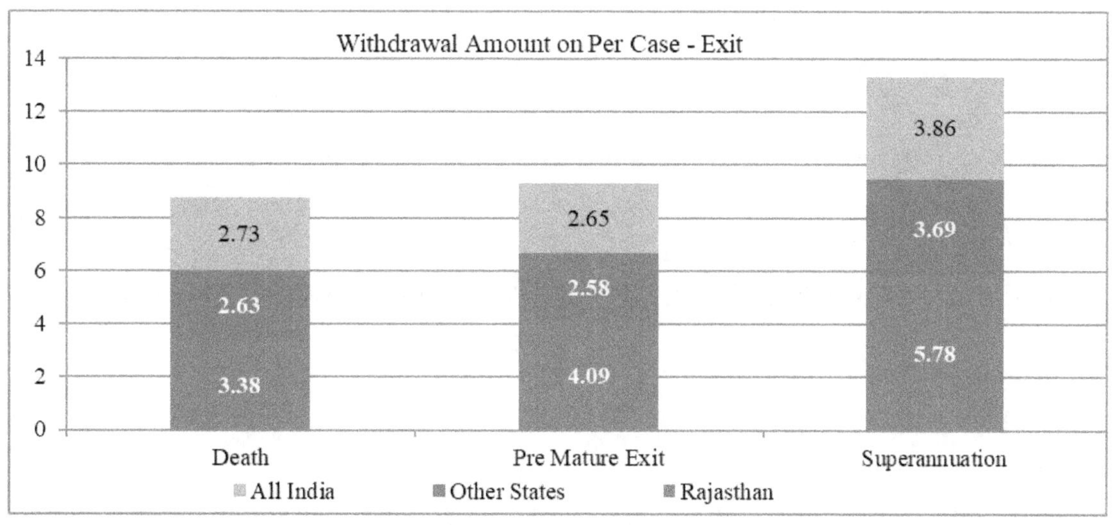

Annuity Purchased by employees from annuity service provider (ASP)

Annuity Service Provider (ASP) is an IRDA registered insurance company empaneled by PFRDA for providing of Annuity Services to NPS subscribers upon their exit from the system. Year 2011 to 2015 all the process of ASP selection to payment processes was done manually. After 2016, online process was picking up speed, although the physical process is still there.

Summary for ASP Details as on 31st March (year Wise since 2011-2012)

Sector	ASP Request to ASP Payment Processed (Offline)	ASP Request to ASP Payment Processed (Since 2011-2012) Post Online submission
Rajasthan	95%	72%
Other States	87%	64%

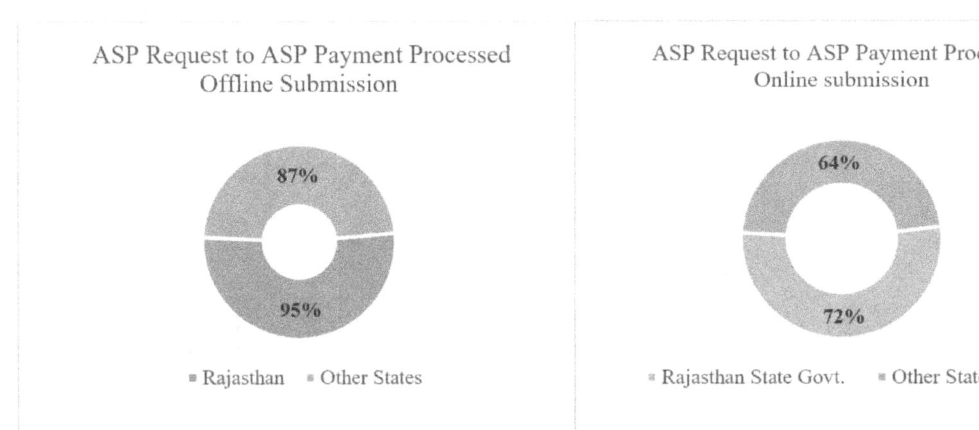

Performance of Rajasthan is better in both online and offline processes.

Online Annuity Pending cases as on November 30, 2019

ASP Name	Sector	Death	Pre-Mature Exit	Superannuation
HDFC Life Insurance Co. Ltd	All India	-	30	326
	Rajasthan	-	-	7
ICICI Prudential Life Insurance Co. Ltd	All India	35	14	182
	Rajasthan	-	-	4
Life Insurance Corporation of India Ltd	All India	204	155	1,646
	Rajasthan	1	4	86
SBI Life Insurance Co. Ltd	All India	125	114	834
	Rajasthan	7	5	95
Star Union Dai-ichi Life Insurance Co Ltd	All India	-	1	4
Total of ASP		**Death**	**Pre-Mature Exit**	**Superannuation**
Rajasthan		8	9	192
All India		364	314	2,992

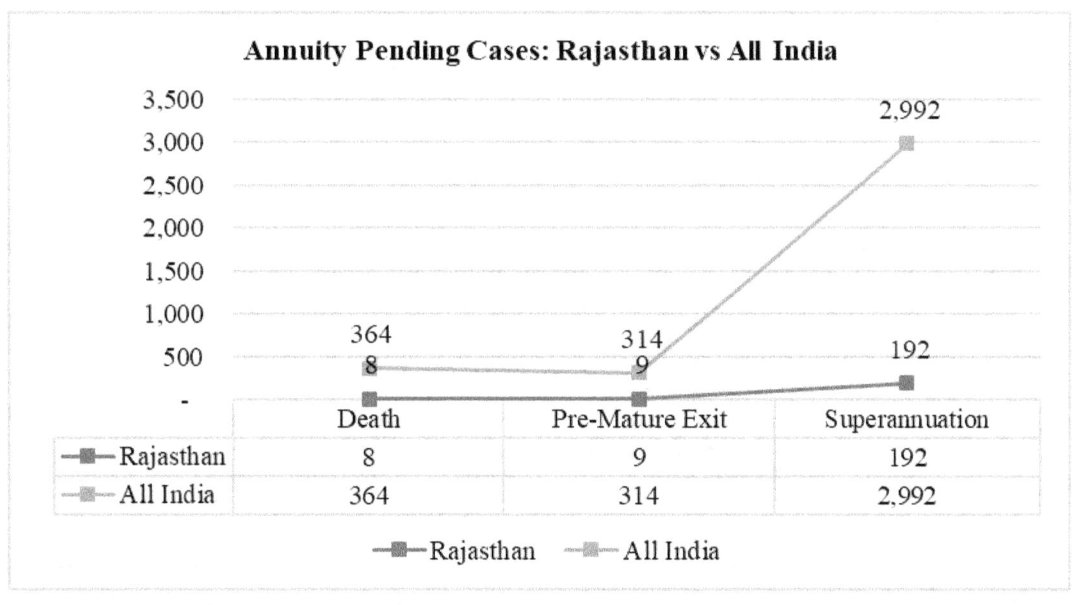

	Death	Pre-Mature Exit	Superannuation
Rajasthan	8	9	192
All India	364	314	2,992

Annuity Purchase by subscribers - NPS-Online
(2016-2017 to 2019-2020)

FY	Number of Subscriber who submitted withdrawal applications (All India)	Number of Subscriber who submitted withdrawal applications (Rajasthan)	Number of Subscriber who have opted for purchase of annuity (All India)	Number of Subscriber who have opted for purchase of annuity (Rajasthan)	Annuity actually purchase by payment to ASP by CRA (All India)	Annuity actually purchase by payment to ASP by CRA (Rajasthan)
2016-2017	7,379	643	3,469	361	622	129
2017-2018	9,233	698	4,589	340	2,654	323
2018-2019	9,893	598	5,355	330	5,408	305
2019-2020	8,245	414	5,709	347	3,737	239
Total	**34750**	**2353**			**12421**	**996**

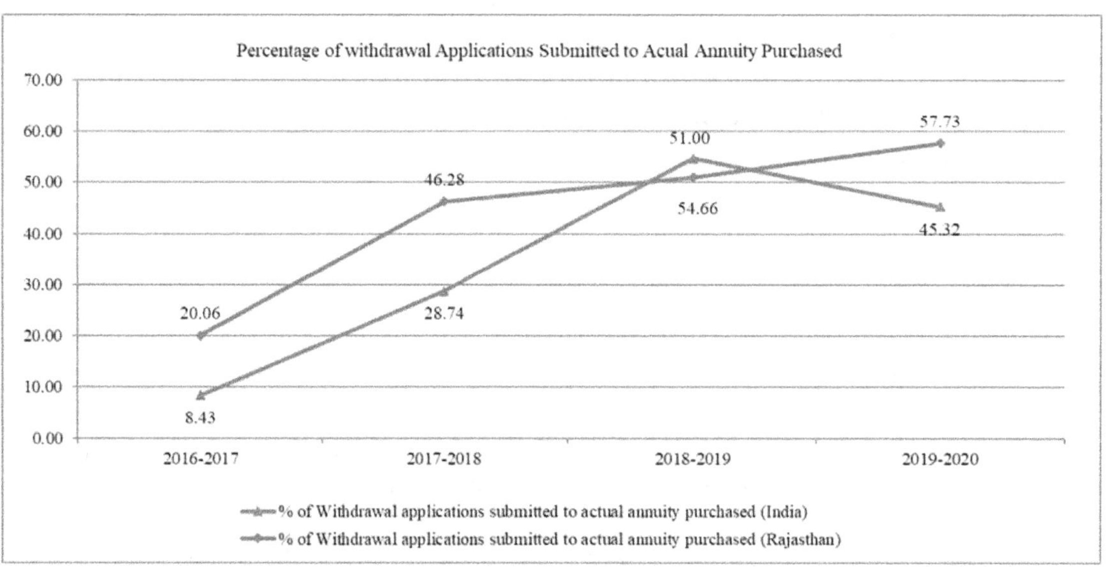

On analyzing the table shown above, it shows that according to NSDL, 50926 employees retired from all State governments between 2011 to 2019 and only 34750 retired employees have submitted withdrawal applications and only 12421 retired employees NSDL have actually made annuity purchases. This means that only 24 percent of the retired employees' annuity was actually purchased between 2011-2019. Almost the same condition is also in Rajasthan, between 2011-2019 total of 3297 employees retired, out of which NSDL have actually annuity purchased only 996 retired employees, which is 30 percent of the total retired employees.

References

- www.sipf.rajasthan.gov.in
- www.ri.org.in
- www.pfrda.org.in
- www.npstrust.org.in
- www.cransdl.orgin
- www.moneycontrol.com

State Investigation Bureau (SIB)
Institutional framework of new generation of tax intelligence through E-

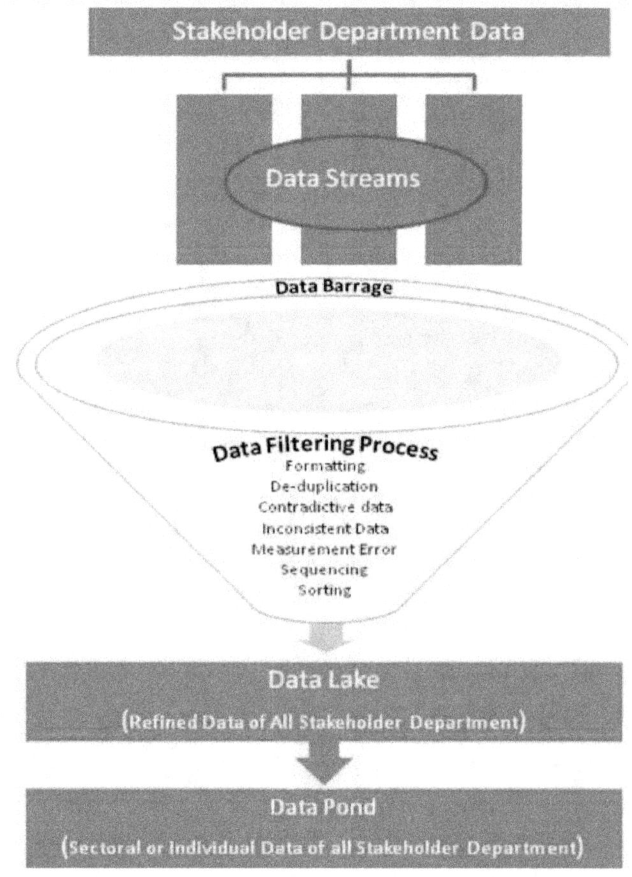

Contents

State Investigation Bureau (SIB) Institutional framework of new generation of tax intelligence through E-networking

Introduction

In the recent past, revenue departments of state governments have focused on online system to cope up with central government online and digitization processes. In this scenario the system of vigilance and intelligence over revenue leakage cannot be based on only the old system of informants and physical interventions. The system of physical intervention generally leads to corruption and harassment for the public at large. Under the federal structure of governance, it is very important that state governments cope up with the centre and other state governments in modernization and information sharing. To improvise the system at state level, a new institution is required to manage, integrate and share financial information with stakeholder departments of centre and state government. The new institution will be named State Investigation Bureau (SIB)

In the era of computerization, institutions should have lean organization; the officials of SIB will appoint on deputation from various fields after special selection. Officials from state government, central government, domain experts and IT experts for collecting, collating, analyzing intelligence and passing it on to the respective stakeholder departments for effective action against revenue leakages. The architecture of SIB covers major revenue earning departments namely, Goods and services tax, Transport, Excise, Mines & Geology and Stamps and Registration, electricity, forest and state local body (stakeholder departments). The institution starts with cases of revenue evasion of stakeholder departments that would be taken in the purview of SIB. SIB is primarily a state government agency and indulges into research and analysis factors affecting tax and nontax revenue of the state. In order to make SIB operational as well as effective, certain amendments are required to be made into the Acts and Rules of the relevant departments to delegate the powers to officers and to enable the officers of SIB to function independently.

It was expected that the officials of SIB would make cases on the qualitative improvement in the intelligence collected from various sources and will hand over the dossier of information to the respective departments for necessary action if required SIB will also take appropriate action in cases where large scale or planned evasion of revenue is detected or more than two departments are involved.

Why is a separate institution at state level required?

1. To cope with other state and centre government ecosystems of information generation and information sharing.
2. Generation of information is very poor because data analysis is at the department level where information from other departments is missing.
3. Limited information exchange between stakeholder departments.
4. Information/ data integration between departments is missing; departments are not willing to share their information with other departments.
5. Departments use different techniques to manage database systems, limited capabilities of available manpower to use data in an efficient

manner and integrate information across departments and also disseminate filtered information.

Key stakeholder departments

> Goods and services tax
>
> State excise
>
> Mining
>
> Registration and stamps
>
> Transport
>
> SIBs of State Governments
>
> Relevant central Government departments, if any

Objectives of State Investigation Bureau (SIB)

1. Reduction of fraud and revenue leakage
2. Deeping of revenue intelligence and data penetration
3. Broadening of tax collection base
4. Real time intelligence sharing
5. Data/ intelligence driven investigation
6. Create a common ecosystem for all states to drive common revenue intelligence and data sharing portal

Scope of State Investigation Bureau (SIB)

1. Create a 360-degree information warehouse with the dissemination of refined information to stakeholder departments.

2. Integrated data repository- Collection of intelligence about all types of evasion and leakages of GST, stamps & registration duties, transport, royalty on mineral and other levies and all other taxes and non-taxes of the state, through systematic survey and collection of information through department records, complaints and from any other source and by any other means.

3. Use modern analytics tools- After scrutiny, analysis, corroboration and consolidation; dissemination of information to concerned departments for necessary action.

4. Continued monitoring and follow up of such cases with the concerned departments, till their logical conclusion.

5. Generate leads for parental departments for smooth functioning.

6. Use information and integrated data management for policy formation and planning.

7. Integration with external data- hassle-free real-time information sharing with central government's departments i.e., NHAI, MCA, GST, Mining, RBI etc.

8. Act as nodal office for FIU(Ind), Regional Economic Intelligence Committee (REIC) and State Level Coordination Committee (SLCC)

9. Powers under various existing statutes will be conferred on Directorate officials for search, seizure and investigation of cases, if found necessary.

Responsibilities of SIB and their officers

1. Collect intelligence about all types of evasion of GST, stamps and registration duties, tax on motor vehicles, royalty on mineral and

other levies and all other tax and non-tax revenue of the State, through systematic survey and collection of information through departmental records, and complaints from any other source.

2. Collect, analyze and process intelligence and its dissemination to the concerned department for effective action against plug revenue leakage.

3. Act as a watchdog over the revenue collection of the State.

4. From the information so collected, make out cases that have large revenue implications, investigate the cases and issue notices to the concerned defaulter and thereafter transfer the case with the concerned department for further necessary action till a logical and final result is achieved.

5. Create and maintain a data warehouse of tax and non tax revenue.

6. Liasoning for enlargement of information with other revenue collecting/investigation organizations/agencies like central DRI, DGGI, Police, Income Tax etc.

Role of Division heads

1. Assigned by Division head REPs are classified into important and general nature.

2. Interaction with the informer and assigning a code number to the informer.

3. Preliminary/Detailed examination of the informer.

4. Recording of the details of the informer including the code number assigned to him in the register of informer's maintained at the level of DG, SIB.

5. Suggest the IO's Surveillance of the target group.

6. Maintenance of record of information gathered from various sources on a file marked as secret and to keep it in personal custody.

7. In case where IO is of the view that he would undertake reconnaissance of the targeted person about the details of such persons including the route map, geographical location of the places accepted to be surveyed/searched.

8. Maintenance of Dossier containing information about the information received from various sources relating to the tax evader.

9. Preparation and submission of satisfactory note to DG, SIB, and warrants of authorization for DG, SIB.

Role of investigation officer of Investigation wing

1. IO of SIB is the initial officer in the SIB, these Officials would be mainly responsible for developing intelligence and also would take up the work of investigation of cases assigned to them.

2. The information received by SIB has been termed as REP (Revenue Evasion Petition). Once a REP is received by any of the modes then the division head allocates the REP to the particular IO. The Officer in charge of the REP register will enter it into the prescribed REP register referred to in the SOP.

3. The uploaded REP will be displayed in the pending task and randomly assigned the REP to the concerned IO by computer aided system.

4. Preparation of warrant of authorization.

5. Assisting in Preparation for conduct of search.

6. Submitting proposals for the grant of reward to the informer

Role of Intelligence officer of Intelligence wing

1. Coordination with IT and domain experts.
2. Well equipped with research skills.
3. Secretary member of the committee on selection of rule.
4. In charge of idea generation to idea selection to dissemination of information to other wings of SIB and other departments.
5. Collaboration with stakeholder departments.

Role of Inspection officer of Inspection wing

1. To enhance ease of doing business with stakeholder departments.
2. To emphasize on systematic changes.
3. Act as a whistleblower for stakeholder departments.
4. Coordination with other wings of SIB.

Manpower Mobilizations

1. Manpower mobilizations

The officials of SIB will appoint on deputation from various fields after special selection. Officials selected from state government, central government, domain experts and IT experts.

➤ Officials from State and Central Government

SIB should be a lean organization consisting of officers/employees from State GST, Mining & Geology, Transport, State Excise and Officers of State Tehsildars Service. To ensure that efficient and upright officers are posted in SIB, the specific rules may prepare for Special Selection and Special Condition of Services for Appointment of persons in State Directorate of Revenue Intelligence. 15% of the monthly basic pay of the officer is paid as a special allowance to the officers who are selected through the above special selection rules.

➤ An official from domain experts

Domain experts will hire from the private sector or hire a retired government official who has expertise in a particular subject on a contractual basis.

➤ IT experts

IT personnel having expertise in the field of data analytics has been sought for SIB.

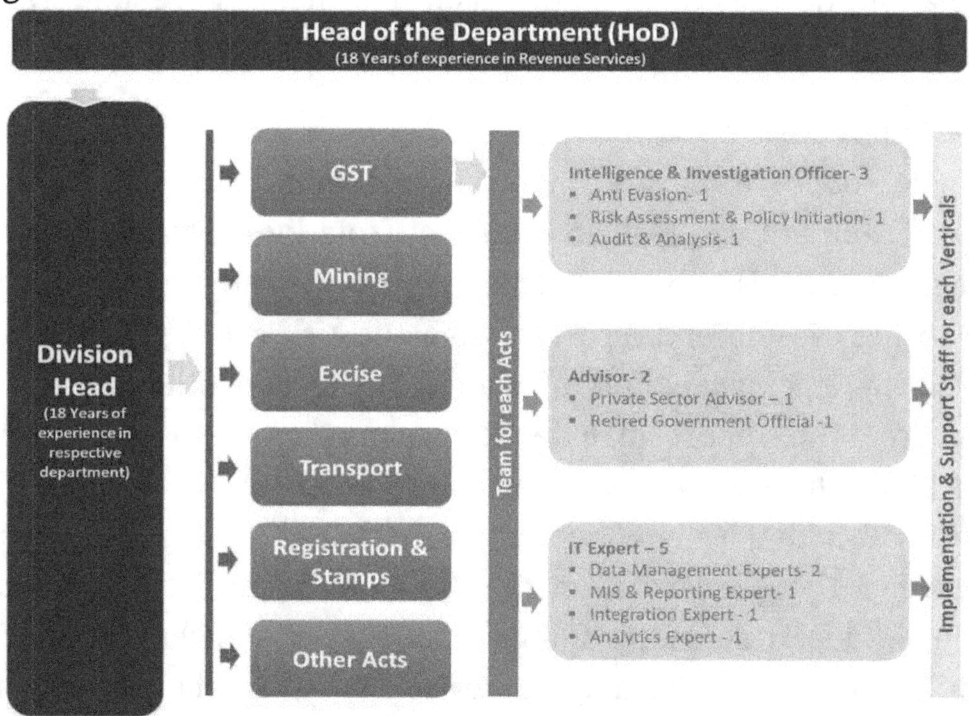

Organizational Structure

SIB should also take up activities other than investigation, specially relating to risk analysis and policy initiatives and tax audit of the cases taken up by the revenue earning departments. Following three independent wings in the SIB: -

1. Investigation wing
2. Intelligence wing
3. Inspection wing

(1). <u>Investigation wing</u>

SIB takes up cases of revenue evasion relating to all stake holder departments. Division head assisted by the officials of the concerned departments posted in SIB. These officials are designated as investigation Officers (IOs) and they have been assigned the powers of investigation of the cases undertaken by them. Revenue evasion petition (REP) related work is done by this wing.

(2). <u>Intelligence wing</u>

Framing of policy is a very important function of the tax revenue administration. SIB can play an important role by analyzing data and creating a mechanism of generating reports relating to the sectors prone to tax evasion and also assessing the risk profile of individual taxpayers by employing tools of data analytics and other sources of intelligence. The report may be known as Suspicious Intelligence Report (SIR). These SIRs may further be classified in three categories, namely A, B and C i.e., moderate risk, risk and of high-risk nature respectively. The above system of SIRs may be devised for all the stakeholder departments. By doing so not only an efficient monitoring system at the level of SIB may be devised but this will also help the parent departments in enhancing their revenues. The risk assessment in those cases where two or more departments are involved can only be made by SIB since officers of all the concerned departments are posted in SIB.

a. Similarly, implication of change in tax rates on enhancement of revenue generation and trends of growth in revenue may also be carried out by SIB for the benefit of decision making at appropriate levels.

b. The above wing shall also be looked into by divisional heads. The reason for doing so is that while performing the task of investigation activities they would be closely associated with the activities of investigation wing and can better appreciate the causes of evasion, risk prone sectors, commodities and about the various measures required to be taken to plug revenue leakages by way of giving appropriate suggestions. The concerned divisional head with the assistance of IOs and personnel of IT posted in SIB or with the assistance of some consultant/advisor working in the field of big data analysis may be allowed to carry out the above task.

(3). <u>Inspection wing</u>

The original functions of tax assessment, creation of demand and disposal cases relating to revenue are performed by the concerned officers of the stakeholder departments. Cases with high stakes are also being dealt with by the concerned officials. To ensure systematic changes and for enhancing "Ease of Doing Business"

In order to contain tax evasion and to inculcate transparency in tax administration, a computerized mechanism has to be developed, wherein certain cases dealt by the concerned authorities may be randomly taken up for audit and analysis by SIB on its own or on the

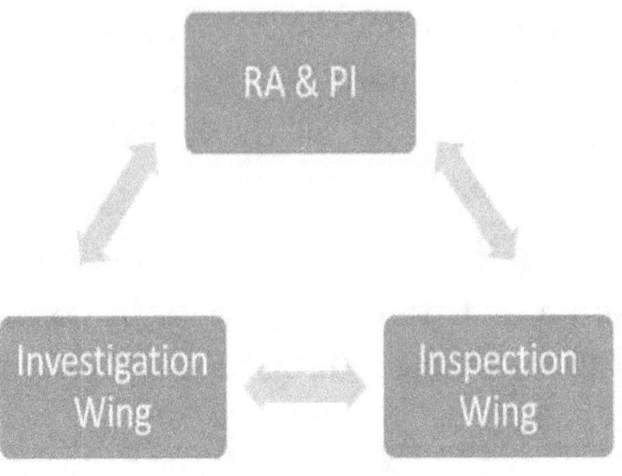

Coordination among IO's of different SIB Wings

directions of the finance department. This wing shall also be looked into by the concerned divisional heads with the assistance of the IOs posted in SIB.

Work flow Structure, functionalities and process

1. **REP module**- A case registered in SIB is known as Revenue Evasion Petition (REP). The REPs are registered on the basis of intelligence received from various sources i.e., from general public, newspapers or from in house intelligence developed by SIB. REPs are classified at the level of SIB in two categories namely, general and important depending on the nature of the case/information received. Besides this the cases developed in-house by the officers are termed as "Suo moto" cases. These cases are developed fully on the basis of exclusive in-house knowledge of the officers. The REP-related work has to be done by the investigation wing.

Revenue Evasion Petition (REP)

1 Receipt of Information

The SIB acts on information that has been received from Public in form revenue evation petition (REP), or on suo-moto cases of IIOs.

A REP can be shared in verbal or written communication either by post, telephone, SMS, online etc

2 Registration of received REP& Suo-moto cases

The received information is registered in the web portal of the SIB.

3 Allocation of registered Cases

Uploaded REPs are then reflected in the system workflow of the division head who then assigns the cases to concerned IIOs.

The IIO examine the issue and decide appropriate line of action on the case.

4 Action Taken Report

IIOs classify the cases in categories such as Important, General, non-concerned and incomplete cases then prepare reports on the Cases and update the findings and action taken.

5 Share Cases with stake holder Departments

Received Cases are then investigated and reports are prepared with specific recommendations . The final reports are shared with DNO for furhter actions.

6 Monitoring of important Cases and closure of REP

Cases forwarded to the DNOs are further followed up by SIB for further progress in the line of demand created and recovered. Final Action Taken Report is required from the DNOs and closer of REP accordingly.

After being assigned by Division head, REPs are classified into important and general nature. After the classification of REP, SIB may retain some of the REPs for investigation at its own level and the rest of the REPs shall be forwarded to the concerned department on their Computer Systems for taking necessary action. The examination and analysis of retained REPs shall be done by the IO. The Action Taken Reports received from the department that the REPs send to them would be examined and analyzed by the IOs and would be sent to the division head on his Computer Network for taking adequate action.

2. **SIR Module-** The selection of the case will be done on the basis of the complete set criteria with the help of computer software. Selection of parameters will be determined by the officers posted in SIB on the basis of their past experience and practice followed by the assessee in the field. The IT experts will identify the case on the basis of these predetermined parameters or rules from the refined data pool of information. The selection of rules is determined by a committee, members of the committee are from stakeholder departments and the member secretary is the intelligence wing of SIB. The SIR-related work was done by the intelligence wing. Determination or Classification of the case will be on the basis of revenue evasion done by the assessee.

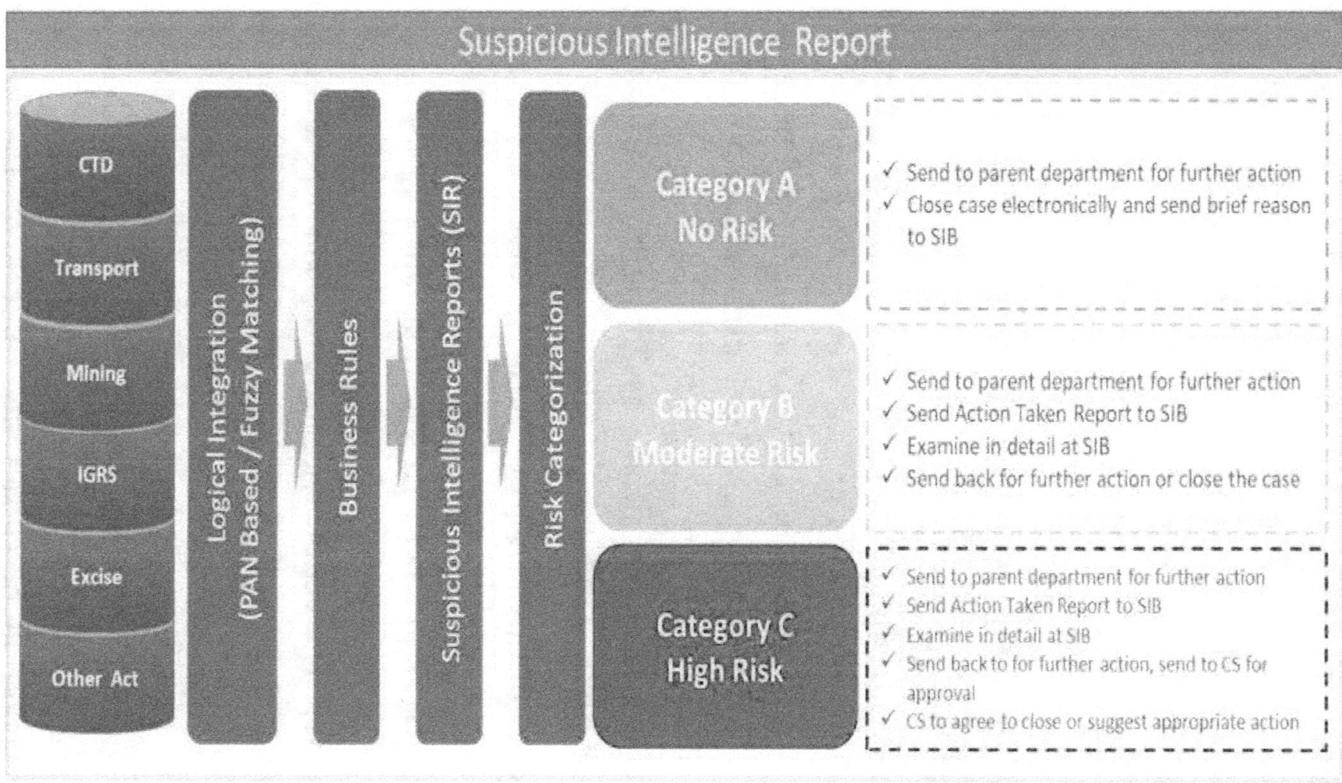

Suspicious Intelligence Report
CTD
Transport
Mining
IGRS
Excise
Other Act
Logical Integration (PAN Based / Fuzzy Matching)
Business Rules
Suspicious Intelligence Reports (SIR)
Risk Categorization
Category A No Risk
Category B Moderate Risk
Category C High Risk
✓ Send to parent department for further action
✓ Close case electronically and send brief reason to SIB
✓ Send to parent department for further action
✓ Send Action Taken Report to SIB
✓ Examine in detail at SIB
✓ Send back for further action or close the case
✓ Send to parent department for further action
✓ Send Action Taken Report to SIB
✓ Examine in detail at SIB
✓ Send back to for further action, send to CS for approval
✓ CS to agree to close or suggest appropriate action

The IT personnel with the assistance of officials posted in SIB having core knowledge of the parent departments will be entrusted with the task of analyzing the data relating to all the stakeholder departments. The report so prepared in each case on the basis of the analysis shall be known as Suspicious Intelligence Report (SIR). These SIRs shall further be classified in three categories, namely A, B and C i.e., moderate risk, risk and high risk nature respectively.

The details of the above-proposed classification of the above SIRs in the three categories are as follows. –

1. **Category A –** In this category those SIRs will be registered which aren't t of a very serious nature. These cases will be sent to the parent departments for further investigation and necessary action. Where the concerned department, after taking appropriate action, is satisfied that adequate action has been taken in the case, may close such cases electronically, assigning brief reasons of closure of the case on the IT system of SIB.

2. **Category B–** In this category, those SIRs will be registered which are of serious nature. These cases will also be sent to the parent departments for further investigation and necessary action. The concerned departments are required to send action taken reports in such cases. The action taken report shall be examined in detail at the level of the SIB. On being satisfied that appropriate action has been taken in the case SIB may close such cases and where it is felt that further action is required to be taken by the department, then such cases shall be sent back to them for taking further action. Hence, it is clear that the cases falling in this category shall only be closed electronically by the SIB and not by the parent departments.

3. **Category C** – In this category, those SIRs will be registered which are of a very serious nature. These cases will also be sent to the parent departments for further investigation and necessary action. The concerned departments are required to send action-taken reports in such cases. The action-taken report shall be examined in detail at the level of the SIB, and on being satisfied that appropriate action has been taken in the case, the matter shall be submitted on file to the Finance Secretary (Revenue) for his approval. If the Finance Secretary (Revenue) agrees to close the case, then such case shall be closed electronically by the SIB and where it is felt that further action is required to be taken by the department then the case shall be sent back to the concerned department for taking further appropriate action in it. Hence, it is clear that the cases falling in this category shall be closed by the SIB subject to the approval of the Finance Secretary (Revenue).

The above system of Suspicious Intelligence Report (SIR) shall be for all the stakeholder departments. By adopting the above system, efficient monitoring by SIB in cases of revenue evasion can be ensured. This will also help the parent departments in enhancing their revenues since with the help of the above team and the officials of all the stakeholder departments posted in SIB the inter-departmental databases shall be used for detection of revenue evasion by SIB which cannot be done by other individual departments.

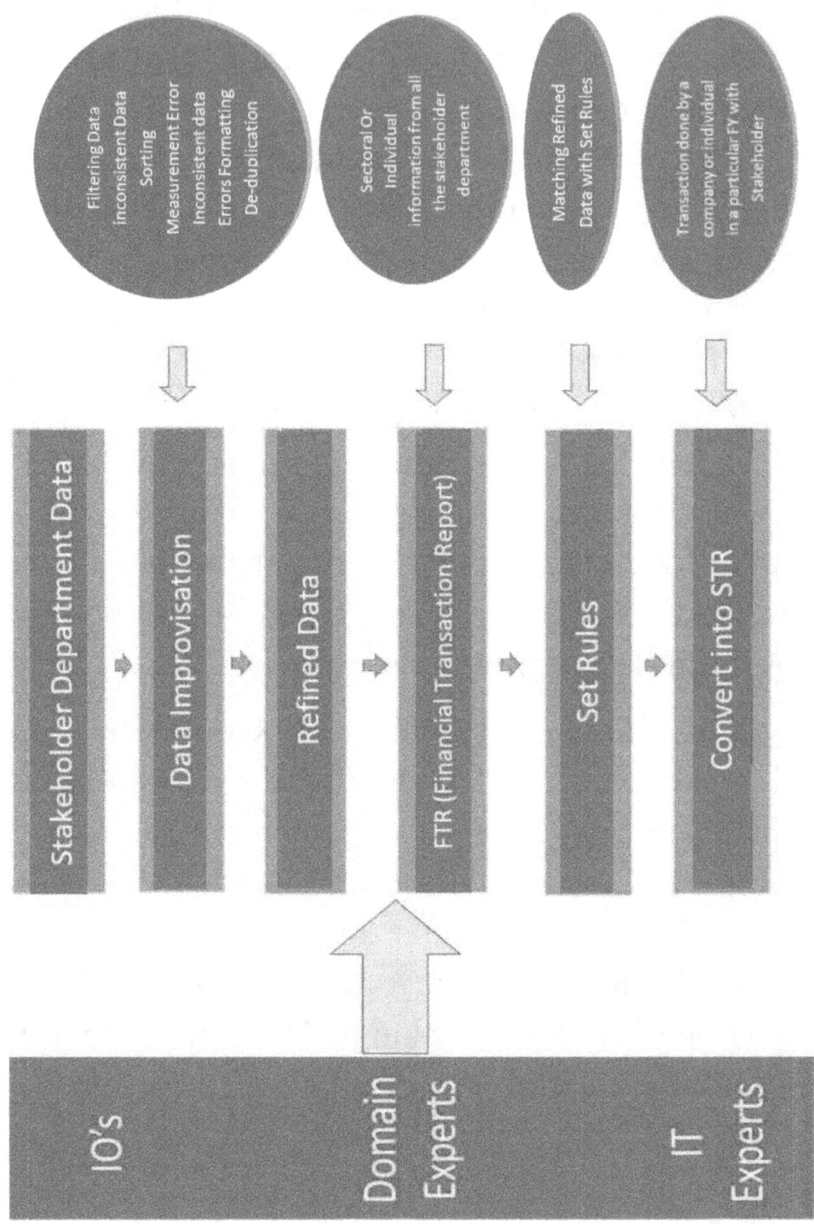

This whole process of preparing of the SIR can be explained in the following way.

- Collection and integration of data of all stakeholder departments.

- Improvisation of data with modern tools.

- Refined data- this is warehouse of data of all stakeholder department.

- Financial transaction report (FTR)- This is a Structured report of a person of a particular financial year in which all information related to stakeholder departments are filled.

- Set rules- Rules are determined by a committee in which all stakeholder departments are members and rules will be determined on the basis of revenue evasion or unexpected trend or movement in the field.

- Suspicious Intelligence Report (SIR) - This is a structured report of a person of a particular financial year, in which rules laid down by committee will be matching with the data lake and FTR will prepare a potential list of persons with complete details of revenue evasion or use of any other method or technique for tax avoidance in all Stakeholder departments.

Suspicious Intelligence Report

Case No.	SIR Type	Actionable	Dissemination details
	A	Departments	Date
	B	GST	Suggested action
	C	Mining	

A. Entity Details

Name		Mining lease No.	
Address		Excise license No.	
PAN		Bank account No.	
GSTN		Vehicle No.	
Nature of		Immovable Property	

Business		detail	
Mobile No.			

B. Reason for Selection

Sr. No.	Departments	Brief Descriptions
1.	GST	
2.	Mining	
3.	Excise	
4.	Transport	
5.	Stamp and Registration	
6.	Electricity	
7.	Forest	
8.	Other Act	

C. Related Parties

Sr. No.	Name of entity	Address	Brief reason
1.			
2.			
3.			

D. Ground of Suspicion

Sr. No.	Departments	Detailed Reason
1.	GST	
2.	Mining	
3.	Excise	
4.	Transport	
5.	Stamp and Registration	
6.	Electricity	
7.	Forest	
8.	Other Act	

E. Other Enforcement Agencies involved

Agency Name	Action already taken	Details shared
		Yes/No

For example, XYZ person in the financial year 2021-22, the following work is not being done as per prescribed rules

1. Transport Department – Purchased a luxury car with complete detail.
2. Excise Department – Owner of liquor showroom with address and any dues etc.
3. Electricity Department – Total bill paid- Rs XYZ.
4. GST Department – Any payment due, return filed, e-way bill detail.
5. Mining Department – Detail of E-Rawanna, mining lease holder address.
6. Stamp & Registrations Department – Property purchase or sale.

System of information sharing across the SIBs of state governments

Committee of members- A committee consisting of all heads of SIBs of different states will meet and discuss policy related issues or any other issues agreed by the other members on a virtual mode, quarterly basis.

Committee of Nodal officer- Every SIB will nominate division head as nodal officer for intelligence sharing and other follow up work. The committee will meet in a virtual mode, monthly basis.

Intelligence Network integration

The intelligence network will provide a highly secured computer aided system to collect requisite data in a synchronized manner from stakeholder departments. Once data is received, data cleaning, sequencing, mining and analysis is required to build 360-degree profiling of and assesses for stakeholder departments. A 360-degree profiling will provide all information of the assessee in a filtered manner like GST return, e-way bills, e-rawana, electricity consummation, purchase or sale of properties, vehicle, details of tenders received, excise liabilities etc. This network will provide the facility of data integration of various departments and provide the analyzed information to IOs and data sharing departments. Intelligence networking will help identify the risk factors and analysis of the data of the assessee/ individual lying with the various source departments. The seamless data exchange with different agencies will also play an important role. This system will yield several benefits like exchange information among other agencies, producing quality inputs, and highlighting revenue leakage. Data fields for capturing data from different revenue departments will be finalized in data template documents.

Due to lack of data sharing between departments, seepage can happen among the system leading to misguided or insufficient information.

Issues	Area of concern	Repercussion	solution
Integration of stakeholder departments software system	➤ Isolated system development ➤ Unavailability of common references	➤ Standardization not achieved ➤ System not able to share information ➤ Delay in processing ➤ Lack of interoperability	➤ Unicode data processing system ➤ Common network architecture ➤
Tax Evasion	➤ Dishonest tax reporting ➤ Lack of centralized data collection ➤ Lack of business process reengineering ➤ Unavailability of latest technology	➤ Delay ➤ Inefficiency ➤ Less transparency ➤ Redundancy	➤ Suspicious intelligence report tracking and monitoring system ➤ Revenue evasion petition ➤ Consolidation and collaboration of stakeholders departments and integrated data networking system

Intelligence networking has three components-

- ➤ Data integration and its access to SIB officers for analyzing the different source data.
- ➤ Centralized web portal containing information SIB.
- ➤ REP and SIR tracking and monitoring system.

This module will provide the facility to the public to lodge complaint/ information about revenue leakage. It will also provide facility to comment on REP to SIB officer and departments.

Use of modern tools of information technology for detection of revenue evasion in stakeholder departments. The advanced analytics capabilities and tools will focus mainly on following areas

a. Creation and maintenance of a data repository which includes data integration of all stakeholder departments and any other external or internal agencies. The access of the database of above departments to the SIB shall be automatic. The nodal agency for it shall be the SIB.

b. Creation of monthly information reports, exception reports and implementation of basic rule-based analytics. The reports of revenue evasion, so generated shall be sent to the concerned departments along with adequate evidence of evasion for necessary action.

c. Implementation of advanced analytics.

d. Assistance for research for policy formulation and Strategic planning.

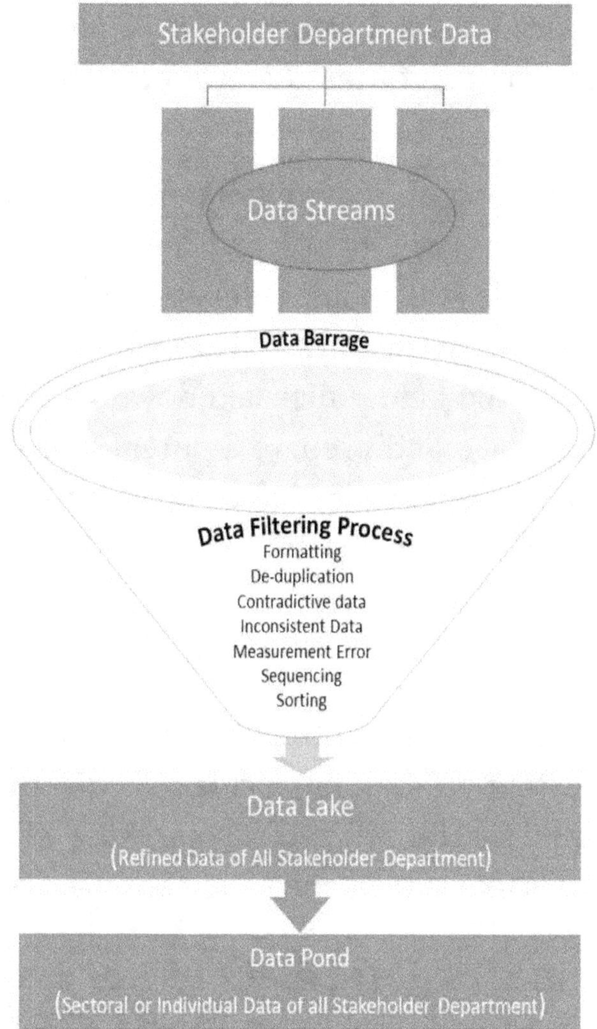

This whole process can be explained in the following way.

1st Stage - Data Stream- collection of data from all stakeholder departments.

2nd stage- Data barrage- integration of data and filtering process.

3rd stage- Data Lake – refined data- at this stage filtered information of all the stakeholder departments of all the assessee is available.

4th stage - Data Pond – refined information of particular company or individual available and information varied from all stakeholder departments.

 Determination of rule-based parameters in which the rules of all stakeholder departments will be there. Rules are determined by a committee in which all stakeholder departments are members and rules will be determined on the basis of revenue evasion or unexpected trend or movement in the field. Rules laid down by the committee will be matching the data lake and prepare a potential list of persons with complete details of revenue evasion or use any other method or technique used for tax avoidance in all Stakeholder departments.

Secret fund

Secret service fund is provided to the SIB for incurring expenditure on secret activities essential for, or incidental to, the work of the investigation wing. It can be utilized for purchase of information and expenses on activities like surveillance and reconnaissance.

Incentive scheme for informers / informants and government employees posted in the SIB

A scheme for grant of reward to informer and government servants should designed to encourage the public to report tax evasion and ensure their participation in the SIB.

Under this scheme, a provision should be made to give an incentive amount to the person giving information on the basis of the importance of the information provided by him to the directorate. This amount is up to maximum of 10 percent of the revenue amount received by the State Government or a maximum of Rs 50 lakh per case whichever is less. The identity of the informant should be kept secret. Under this scheme, a provision should also be there to give incentive amount to the officers/employees working in the SIB. This incentive amount will be payable to those government officers/employees, who will have a special contribution in uncovering the cases of revenue evasion and in such cases the revenue receipt will be Rs. 50 lakh or more. Individually the amount in one case is maximum Rs. 50,000 / - and working as a team, the team will get a maximum of Rs.2.00 lakh per case. The maximum amount in the scheme for government servants of Rs. 20.00 lakhs.

The informer can register his complaint/information electronically or in writing to the SIB.

The information submitted or the cases made by the officials of SIB on their own are assigned a unique number and is termed as Revenue Evasion Petition (REP).

Challenges

Limited information exchange between different Revenue departments of the state.

Data available in silos, power of integration is missing that needs an integrated information repository.

Need to look beyond what insights are provided by the stakeholder department.

Limited capabilities in using data quality and fuzzy logic for integration of information across departments.

Need of a single source of truth to provide an integrated and consistent view.

Lack of facilities to disseminate insightful information at the field level and vice versa.

Evolving and changing department requirements.

Lack of facilities to disseminate insightful information at the field level and vice versa.

Suggestions and requirements

The use of advanced analytics should be done in such a way that it incorporates both legal and business scenarios which identifies the existing data gaps, evaluates potential revenue leakages and calculates the risk scores of the probable tax evader on a continuous basis. To achieve this, it is required to hire a skilled technical team/consultant which support SIB by providing training and skill upgradation of the personnel of the SIB and support to use Advanced Analytics. Team also suggests modalities for establishment and management of data analytics & Business Intelligence function/systems.

For efficient functioning SIB must fulfill or setting up following-

i. Data access of multiple revenue earning departments like GST, Transport, Mining, IGRS, Excise etc. would be provided to SIB.

ii. Utilization of existing advanced analytics provided by the IT department of the State Government (Infra and software).

iii. Identify analytics scenarios, prioritize analytics scenarios and plan implementation accordingly.

iv. Implement application software for data integration, data quality, analytics, reporting, and advanced visualization etc.

v. Identification of sources of data and required data for analysis in collaboration with the department officers.

vi. Rule-based or analytics-based, the consultant is required to deliver a detailed approach note, user acceptance criteria, test criteria, design documentation and the developed and tested.

vii. Create a single data repository and data analytics with data sourced from all stakeholder departments and other internal/external data sources as available.

viii. Historical data, incrementally updated data, and other information as required for data analytics or MIS scenarios.

ix. Perform data Integration of various identified sources.

x. Data quality assurance by way of data profiling, data de-duplication, and clustering based on various data rules and combinations.

xi. Creation/update of conceptual, logical, and physical data models for the central data repository.

xii. Perform necessary transformations to the source data.

xiii. Configuration of business rules/scenarios including designing algorithms for the identified leakage scenarios.

xiv. Development of dashboard using advanced visualization capabilities.

xv. Implementation of analytics models/fraud detection models/ risk models as required for the departments using AI/ML techniques.

xvi. Provide technical support for any changes or enhancements for developed application components.

xvii. Capacity- usage of analytics capabilities by imparting training of stakeholder departments after set-up and operationalization of analytics application.

SIB may be authorized to use CDR analysis software and intercept calls of syndicates of suspected tax evaders. By doing so the activities of tax evaders may be tracked for effective check on tax evasion.

Adequate facility for creating lockups for keeping persons arrested for the evasion of GST and Excise duty and authorizing Director General, SIB to exercise the powers of sanctioning arrest of the evaders under Goods & Services Tax Act, 2017.

Sharing of information and power to investigate the economic offences relating to taxes lying in the domain of the State Government. The criminal liability may be looked into by the police whereas the economic liability may be looked into by SIB in coordination with police.

Wagonomics after breakthrough of demonetization

Contents

Wagonomics after breakthrough of demonetization

Introduction

In India around 450 million workers engaged in the unorganized sector are facing deep trouble after demonetization. The impact of economic changes daunting the micro and small industries drastically spillover on unskilled or semi-skilled through wage cut to job cut. The three main milestone policy decisions in the recent Indian economy, which totally destroyed the nitty gritty of wagonomics in India are Demonetization, Goods and Service Tax (GST), and Lockdown. The impact of each incident is different on the socio-economic conditions of the daily wage earner, migrant workers and marginalized workers, which is categorized in three zones namely red zone, Grey zone and Brown zone.

Policy measures

> ➢ Demonetization on 8th November, 2016 defined as 'leg breaker'.

> ➢ Implementation of Goods and Services Tax on 1st July, 2017 along with amendment of Benami transaction (Prohibition) act, Black money act and RERA defined as 'back breaker'.

> ➢ Lockdown implemented from 23rdMarch, 2020 defined as 'neck breaker'.

Wage earners are categorized in three different Zones

> ➢ Red Zone- This zone consists of a major population of unskilled workers but semi-skilled or skilled laborers are also there depending on the socioeconomic background of the worker.

- ➢ Grey Zone- Workers who fall in the category are generally semi-skilled workers, they have some training and skill but not enough to do specialized work.
- ➢ Brown Zone- In this category most of the workers are generally skilled workers, some of them are semi-skilled workers.

Further, we discuss the impact of the above policy decision taken by the government on various zones of workers.

Why we have called above three measures hurdles for the economy or breakers for the front runner of the economy known as a laborer-

- ➢ **Demonetization** stopped the wheels of the economic activities completely due to sudden restrictions on withdrawals, worried people about spending, and made industries anticipate an economic slowdown. Demonetization's major impact was the slowdown of the growth rate of the economy. The worst affected sectors were the construction, hospitality, tourism, textile, and automobile sectors.

  The direct and indirect impacts of the slowdown on the workers in the different zones vary differently due to their socio-economic conditions. The degree of impact of each incidence was different for different zones of workers. Demonetization impacted all workers in different zones heavily and seized the wheels of the economic activities and also the poor households. People wasted time in long queues, the liquidity crisis in the informal economy, and the rural market activities slowed down. The base of the MSME composed of an informal sector, which is based on cash-based transaction, in this condition the market of

MSME was seized for more than a quarter or so. As per Jean Drèze, "demonetization in the booming economy is like shooting at the tire of a racing car". Further, he added, that the sudden move of demonetization creates a scary situation for people who live on the margin of subsistence.

➢ **Goods and Service Tax** combination with amendment of Benami transaction (Prohibition) act, Black money act and RERA, proved as 'backbone breaker' for the economic activity and for the workers of the economy. The backbone of the manufacturing sector is Micro, small and medium enterprise (MSMEs) which was still struggling to recover from the demonetization move when GST had come into existence. The consequences of demonetization and GST seems to have broken the Indian economy's back because it came at a point when the Indian economy was already in a weak condition. The GST further delayed the recovery process of economic activities which were already slow, in the time when industries or their workers were not recovered properly, which seems to have broken down the back of economic activity.

➢ **Lock down** was enforced ruthlessly at a short notice, leaving in crisis millions of workers who had to march hopelessly back to their villages. Wage earners were not getting time to settle their family safely, but they were forced to stay at the government's arrangements for them. Workers did not understand what to do in such a situation. It meant that workers were in double trouble because social distancing was not maintained in slums and in the cities. Also, they were made to reach a situation of starvation since food and basic health facilities depended on government efficiency. Laborers were very badly affected by demonetization and GST and other tax laws implemented during this period. In this situation of lockdown, a sudden stop of economic activities again screwed the weaker section of the society from all aspects of their life. It is as if the weaker section's life is on the ventilator. In this sense, lockdown is defined as a 'neck breaker' for the weaker section of society. Around 53 percent of the rural workers are self-employed, around 25 percent are casual workers in the economy, and most of the self-employed workers are solo workers in their business. They lost faith in the surroundings which were not controlled by them or the policies which were not directly imposed or targeted for workers, affecting them in a cascading way. The cascading effect on unorganized sectors like daily wage earners is going to worsen.

Impact of above breakers on the key labor-intensive sectors of the economy

Workers spread across the sectors of the economy. There were around 450 million workers in India, of these, 94 percent work in the unorganized sector. Workers in the textile industries are around 45 million, iron and steel industries are around 2.5 million, petrochemical industries are around 2.2 million, automobile industries are around 1.7 million, direct and indirect workers in the construction sector are around 40 million, and hotel and restaurant sector make up around 7.5 million. Most of them are migrant workers and marginalized workers.

> **Textile industry-** Impact of demonetization on the textile sector- Major part of the textile industry under the unorganized sector consists of handlooms, handicrafts, small and medium mills. Almost 70 to 80 percent of workers are paid weekly wages in cash. The majority of workers are migrants and do not have bank

accounts. Textile industries are not able to pay their workers' wages in cash after demonetization. Textile production got severely affected due to the liquidity crisis and most of the workers left for their villages.

On the GST front, the primary difficulty was to take input credit. The frequent changes in rules and regulations created uncertainty among the industry, which lead to lower production in the coming months and the implementation of GST.

And, during the lockdown, production was totally stopped and workers were in big trouble as most of the workers in this segment are migrants and daily wage earners.

➢ **Construction sector-** Impact of demonetization on construction sector- The industry consists of about 10 percent of GDP and 40 million of employment through direct or indirect manners.

Due to demonetization many projects stopped, industry could not make cash payments to the marginal workers because of restrictions on withdrawal limits. Also causing people to be wary of spending and property registration decreased up to 40 percent.

GST has simplified the tax treatment for the industries and resolved long pending issues. The significant benefit appears to be an increase in input credit on the procurement of goods and services. Do away with the multiple taxes but cumbersome process of GST and confusion often associated with the process, the exemption of stamp duties and registration charges that burden the buyer mitigates the input tax credit benefits.

And, during the lockdown, work was totally stopped and workers were in big trouble as most of the workers in this segment are migrant and daily wage earners.

> **Iron and steel industry-** Iron and steel are primary requirements of the construction industry and are commonly used in manufacturing machine parts. Demonetization impacted the secondary steel sector as most of the business conducted by mini-mills, rolling factories is cash-based. Weak demand and the rising cost of raw materials like coal during that time affected the industries badly. An anticipated slowdown in the real estate sector on account of the demonetization drive affected the demand of steel.

GST would initially have a higher cost due to transition and increase in working capital requirement, but in the long run will be beneficial, in view of lower tax on input under GST. The trend in this sector was that transactions were usually done through cash mode. Cash mode is quick and on the spot and easy to proceed.

And, during the lockdown, work was totally stopped and workers are in big trouble as most of the workers in this segment are migrant and daily wage earners.

Wage-earners are described in three different categories

> Red Zone or dark zone – workers who fall in this category are very vulnerable. This zone consists of a major population of unskilled workers but semi-skilled or skilled laborers are also there depending on the socio-economic background of the

worker. Unskilled worker refers to those workers who have no special training or experience in a particular field. Their average wages range between Rs. 5000/- to Rs. 7000/- rupees. These workers are typically found in positions of manual labor such as packers, assemblers or loaders. Unskilled workers consist of construction laborers, parking attendants, cleaners, farm workers etc. Between 200 to 300 million workers are in this category. Basic features of the category are as under-

- ✓ Mostly workers are unskilled.
- ✓ Workers with no immovable assets and very few moveable assets.
- ✓ No savings and obviously no investments.
- ✓ Mostly migrant workers.
- ✓ Mostly worker shelter at workplace.
- ✓ Their education and health conditions are in poor shape.
- ✓ Generally, workers are out of the government social security net as they have no fixed address and lack information about government schemes.

➢ Grey Zone- Workers who fall in the category are generally semi-skilled workers, they have some training and skill but not enough to do specialized work. Average wages ranging between Rs. 7,000/- to Rs. 10,000/-. Semi-skilled workers examples are painters, drivers, waiters, security guards, back-office workers, house or office peons. Around 75 to 125 million workers are in this category. Basic features of the category are as under-

- ✓ Workers with no or very few immovable assets at their native place.

- ✓ Mostly workers are staying at site or rented accommodation near the site.
- ✓ They hold small savings.
- ✓ Mostly workers are migrants from villages.
- ✓ Generally, workers understand the value of government schemes but due to less or inadequate information, with fa frequent job change or address change, this group could not benefit from government schemes.

- ➢ Brown Zone- In this category most of the workers are generally skilled workers, some of them are semi-skilled workers. Petty contractors, nurses, tailors, sales representatives, travel agents, small agents, or riders in new online platforms come under this zone. Their average wage ranges between Rs. 1000/- to Rs. 15000/-. Around 20 to 40 million workers are in this category. Basic features of the category are as under-

- ✓ Skilled worker.
- ✓ They have some immovable and moveable property at native place and may be at cities where they are working.
- ✓ They have rented accommodation.
- ✓ They are aware of government schemes.

Impact of various policy breakers on wage earners in a different zone

This diagram is mainly divided into three zones, namely Red zone, Grey zone, and Brown zone reflecting the present income of the workers on the X-axis and expected income after six months on the Y-axis.

To better understand the diagram, various policy breakers are summarized in tabular format.

	Red Zone	Grey Zone	Brown Zone
Demonetization	P-P1	Q-Q1	R-R1
Goods and Service Tax	P1-P2	Q1-Q2	R1-Q1#
Lock down	P2-P3	Q2-P1*	Q1-Q2

* Point where wage earners of Grey zone are entered in Red zone.

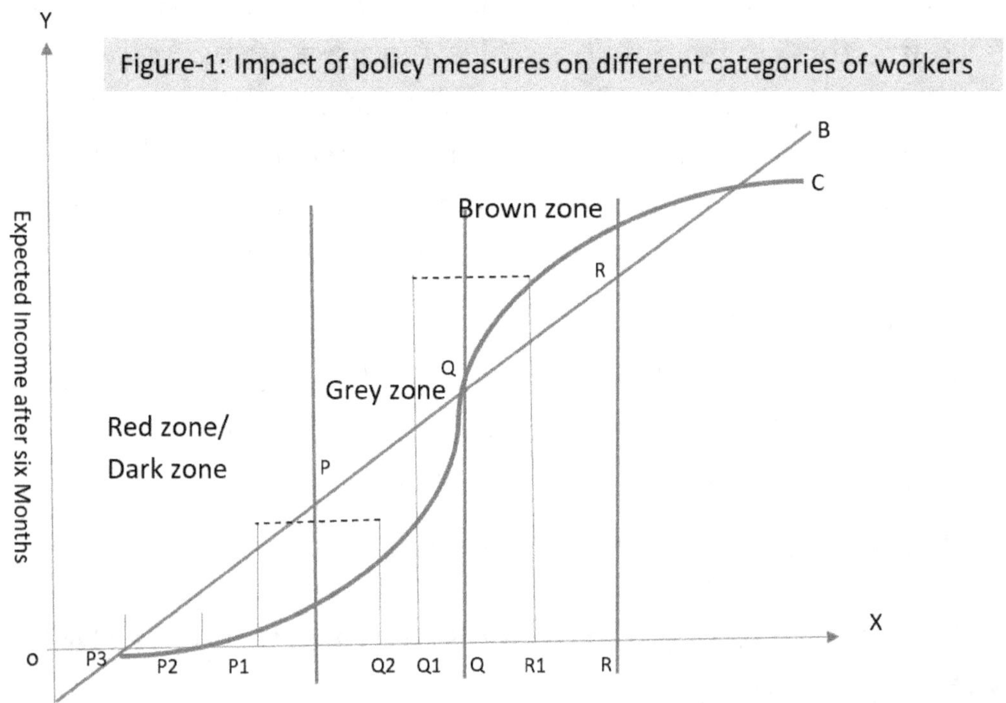

Point where Brown zone workers are entered in Grey zone.

P

OX- Income in present days

OY- Expected income after six months

OB- Income is equal in present days and after six months

OQC- actual Income

O to P – Red Zone

P to Q – Grey Zone

Q to R – Blue Zone

Impact of various policy breakers on wage earners in Red zone

➤ Impact of demonetization-

Before demonetization industries were doing good (not at their best), wage earners were expected to save some money for their future prospects and necessary items. After demonetization, in this zone, labors were shunted out, new industries were badly affected, labor intensive industries were either closed down or their production slowed for a few months with less labor. Bargaining power of unskilled labor was very low, resulting in an unexpected decline in wages.

The wage earners of this zone were still hopeful that the impact of demonetization is going to be good, as was the picture shown by the political leaders. They somehow managed their families' basic needs during this time and started getting jobs on lower wages. The demonetization slowed the production of industries, lowered the speed of growth, resulting in shattered dreams of the poor of the betterment of their future.

In the figure-1, Red zone ranges between point O to P. When demonetization was introduced the income of the worker, which is, at present, at point P reduced to point P1. P1 is the point where the worker is only able to manage food two times a day for the family.

Shifting from P to P1 also shows that the worker has less income than what he was having before the demonetization.

The demonetization on red zone in a nutshell-

- ✓ They lost their job.
- ✓ They lost their shelter as workers are staying at sites where they are working.
- ✓ Lost their little bargaining power which they have as labor union.
- ✓ Unskilled laborers were sheltered in kacchi basti in the big cities and stopped dreaming for the future but were still hopeful of their future.

➢ Impact of goods and services tax (backbreaker)

Most of the small industries opened within one year before demonetization were closed down, the surviving companies could not compete with the bigger ones due to GST as it increased their basic cost of maintenance of the new indirect tax regime. As per figure-1, With the introduction of GST, the workers' income is further reduced and reaches point P2 from P1. At this point, the worker is struggling to arrange one-time food for a day for the family,

Impact of GST on red zone in a nutshell

- ✓ After demonetization, laborers who started working on lesser wages were also in trouble.
- ✓ For survival, the red zone families took more loans to meets their both ends.
- ✓ No proper two meals a day for the red zone families.
- ✓ Expectation of a better future lost somewhere in the complexity of the new tax regime.

- ✓ The red zone families were indulged in the bad/ illegal work and habits.
- ➢ Impact of lockdown

When the honorable PM announced a lock down with only a four-hour prior notice, the red zone workers were the most affected people in this country. The lockdown was enforced ruthlessly by selecting such a short notice. Wage-earners did not get enough time to settle their family where they felt safe, and were forced to stay at government facilities. Around 150-200 million red zone workers did not understand what to do in this condition. This meant that workers were in double trouble because social distance was not maintained in slums in the cities, also they were reached a starvation situation where food and basic health depended on government efficiency.

As per figure -1 the point P2 to P3 shows the impact of the lockdown. This is the starvation point for the workers. Though it is above the point O but workers income is almost zero.

Impact on red zone in nutshell

- ✓ Lost their job.
- ✓ Lost shelter again and this time shelter provided by government for time being.
- ✓ Their survival completely depended on government machinery for distribution of cooked food.
- ✓ They lost their hope for any job in future.
- ✓ Basically, red zone people had to beg in front of the so-called charitable institutions or people for food. This was the new normal after the lockdown, that they had to accept begging as the only solution for survival.

Impact of various policy breakers on wage earners in Grey zone

There were around 100 million workers in this zone just before demonetization, and filled the economic space of semi-skilled laborers. Their life was going in a routine manner in the big towns or cities before demonetization, with the future expectation to buy some basic moveable assets where they are working and also better education for their kids.

> Demonetization- On 8th November, 2016 announcement of demonetization was a big hammer on their confidence and also on their future planning. Most of the workers lost their jobs for a few months, then returned to their native places. They lost their savings for routine expenses during the period of unemployment.
>
> When they returned to work places, the scenario was a bit changed as factories/ industries etc. were trying to survive through cost cuttings. In this picture many blue zone workers also tried to manage in the grey zone because blue zone people also lost their jobs substantially. In the figure-1, after demonetization the worker's income reduced from point Q to Q1. This shifting from Q to Q1 shows more gap between the workers' today's income and expected future income.

Impact of demonetization in a nutshell

- ✓ Lost jobs for a few months after demonetization, returned to native places.
- ✓ They lost their saving during unemployed period.

- ✓ When they again returned to the work places due to inter-zone competition and strategy of cost cutting through less wages or job cuts by the factories, laborers got lower wages.
- ✓ They consume their savings for daily bread. The dreams of betterment were ruined after this incident.
- ✓ Workers of this zone were more aware of government schemes.
- ✓ More than one fourth of the grey zone workers entered into the red zone market.

- ➢ Goods and Service Tax- The complicated indirect tax regime on the part of daily changes in the rules and regulations hampered the economy. New businesses and industries did not survive and established companies survived but their cost of production increased.

In this scenario, workers of the grey zone in the real estate sector were most affected due to double trouble with RERA. Old projects had slower growth and no new projects started after GST and RERA.

In figure -1, due to GST, wages reduced from point Q1to Q2

Impact of GST in nutshell-

- ✓ Grey zone workers lost their jobs and they entered into the Red zone labor market for jobs and managed to get jobs with lower wages. By this act, red zone workers who were already in bad condition reached the point of starvation.
- ✓ Now workers in this zone were staying in the site or slums where they were working. They shifted from rented accommodations which were in good condition.
- ✓ Lost faith in the future prospects.
- ✓ Most of them sold their moveable assets they have in the cities.

- ➤ Lock Down- While reaching

- ➤ March 2020, the population of this zone was reduced to 50 million from 60 million, as other workers forcefully shifted to the red zone after demonetization and GST.

As per figure-1, worker's wages come to point P1 from Q2. This is the point where they come into the red zone where workers can only manage two times food a day for the family.

Impact of lock down in nutshell

- ✓ During lock down, factories and other business premises closed down so shelter at the site were also closed, so they shifted to slums or government-identified places.
- ✓ During the first phase of the lock down, half of them managed to escape from government-identified places and reached their native place or were detained on inter- state borders by state administration.
- ✓ With no savings and no wages, the people of this zone started selling their assets in the village.
- ✓ Hope for future prospects is totally ruined.

Impact of various policy breakers on wage earners in Brown zone

- ➤ Demonetization- There were around 30-40 million workers in this group before demonetization. Before demonetization, there were many new schemes to develop skills in the workers of unskilled or semi-skilled workers. After skill development programs and other initiatives, the horizon of the blue zone was increased substantially. But the training and skill given to the worker was not enough to provide them a job in skilled labor markets. In the market, unskilled and semi-skilled workers who got trained in a particular sector produced his/ her self as skilled workers and demanded wages accordingly. After the announcement of demonetization, the work force under blue zone got seriously affected because of the elastic nature of their work. They lost their jobs mainly in hotel and restaurant industries, automobile and petrochemical industries.

Workers lost their jobs and agreed to work on less wages or switched to a semi-skilled work profile.

As per figure -1 their wages reduced from R toR1

Impact of demonetization in nutshell

✓ This zone worker lost their jobs for a few months, after that managed to work on lesser wages or either work in the grey zone.

✓ Workers consumed their major chunk of savings in day-to-day expenses, during the settlement period after demonetization.

✓ It was difficult for them to deposit EMI or other installment during this period which resulted in selling moveable property at lower price.

✓ One fourth worker of this zone entered into the grey market.

➢ Goods and Service Tax- After new indirect tax regime, companies were much more aware and started calculating per worker production, in this background the skill development programs started by the center and state government were practically review by the market forces and the new entrant in the market from the red or blue zone were pushed back to their places or worse one.

As per figure -1, after the GST implementation, wages reduced to such an extent that it's one big segment of brown zone workers entered into grey zone at point Q1 from R1.

Impact in GST in nutshell-

- ✓ Blue zone workers struggled in the market. Only experienced or well-trained workers survived with lower wages.
- ✓ Workers newly entered in this zone, mostly left as their qualification and ambitions were not matched with the market forces.
- ✓ Most of the newly entrants of this zone again entered in the grey zone market or even red zone market.
- ✓ Experienced workers of this zone have liabilities of EMI and other family responsibilities. They had no option but to sell their assets after demonetization and GST.

- ➢ Lock Down- The index of industrial production (IIP) was moving in a lower direction before lock down. The lock down has impacted very hard on this zone as the economy is almost closed for more than 40 days. As per studies, GDP is going to decline by 30 percent. As per figure -1, after the lockdown announcement wages reduced to Q1-Q2.

Impact of lock down in nutshell

- ✓ After lock down uncertainty is zooming on the head of this group.
- ✓ Living standard of the family is going down.
- ✓ Selling of their properties in the villages is going to happen.

✓ Expectations of the future are not clear in their mind, whether they are going to start their own business or work in the blue zone market or in the grey market.

Conclusion/ Suggestions-

The series of policy decisions since demonetization has worst hit the informal sector workers, migrant workers in the cities and small businessmen. Basically, to maintain one's job, sustain respectable wages and collective bargaining power are the weakest points at this time period.

After lockdown, Centre and State Governments have announced various relief packages through PMGKY's direct cash transfer, free ration for BPL families, 24 percent of wages transferred to EPF for the wage earner whose monthly salary is less than 15,000/-etc. The Ministry of Labor has decided to distribute available cess funds under Building and other construction workers (BOCW).

But the biggest challenge is effective implementation of the welfare measures. The aim of PMGKY's 1.7 lakh crore packages was to reach out to all class of the poor, but migrant workers are generally floating population and are least informed about the government schemes. Migrant workers are in least priority under policy formation of urban local bodies, hence, they do not have voting card, address proof or any other recognition proof from the urban authorities. So, their ration card from native place will not work in the city, no integration of AADHAR with ration cards are hurdling points before the government. During lockdown, migrants were given an option to apply for E-coupon or temporary ration cards. The lockdown has exposed the points where the government should work upon. As a temporary worker, they are not welcomed by the urban societies, so they are excluded from government facilities and social security net by the urban local bodies. Local political leaders ignored them because they do not have voting rights in the urban area. Due to temporary nature of their work arrangement, they are not part of the trade unions, that is why their basic work-related issues are not in their favor, like working hours, workplace condition, compensation, welfare benefits provided by the employers. If migrant labor gets recognition by the urban local bodies and trade unions than their most basic issues are resolved. State government and local bodies should recognize the unorganized sector workers in their policy formation.

93 percent of Indian labor work under the unorganized sector, where most of the workers are hired through contractors, even workers do not know their actual employer and they are generally not registered under the Employees' Provident Fund Organization (EPFO). Only formal or organized sector workers are registered as members of the EPFO. When 93 percent workers are out of EPFO network then the policy decision of 24 percent of wages transferred to EPF for the wage earner whose monthly salary is less than 15,000/- is much workable for unskilled laborers. The need of the hour is the speedy increase of the formalization of the labor market, so that they can benefit from EPFO schemes.

The cess fund collected under the Construction Welfare Fund (CWF) under the Building and Other Constructions Workers Act, 1996, is around 520 billion. Under the BOCW act registered workers are around 35 million. The benefits include pension, assistance in case of accident, housing loan, group insurance premium, medical expenses etc. and so on. But, after so many years of implementation, still the Act is very poor. Construction workers welfare boards are constituted by the State

Governments and even after so many years of their formation, they are not in working conditions.

So, funds collected under this act are not distributed properly. The basic issue of implementation of the act is registration, collection and distribution of funds. Only 50 to 60 percent of construction workers are registered, workers are not aware of the act. Most small construction sites are avid to pay cess, but there is no sound mechanism to collect the cess under this act. The online registration of workers and allotting a unique identification number will help the workers but the process of issuing a unique number is very slow. The decision of distribution of available cess funds under Building and other construction workers (BOCW) does not cover many of migrant workers and workers who work in small sites.

<u>Universalization of PDS</u>- The PDS scheme should be mechanized with the incorporation of different aspects of the holistic meal. The National Food Security Act, 2013, provides the right to food to the citizens of the country. Although the act covered almost every aspect of food security but in reality, food basket is filled with grains, pulses, oil and minor nutrients which are not available.

<u>Strengthening of MGNREGA</u>- The coverage under this act should be wider. The act is applied on unskilled manual work only. It should be expanded to other skilled areas of works related to farmers and artisans. In this scheme, when other than manual works are started then semi-skilled or skilled workers also get employment in the rural area. Capacity building of panchayats and local bodies is very much required. Infrastructure building of basic amenities like sanitation, drinking water, schools and hospitals should be covered under this act.

To restore confidence in the workers, Government and industries must take immediate policy decisions which empower the labor with good health and education. Government should give thrust to the Right to Education (RTE) act and improve the infrastructure of government schools. On the health front, Mohalla clinics should be opened in labor dense areas. BOCW act and MGNERGA are required for better implementation. In the industry sector, the CSR funds should be utilized in education, health and sanitation aspects of the workers.

Wage vigilance system- The situation of wage earner after COVD is miserable due to prices of food baskets, huge loans and fear of future. It is time to enforce the idea of living wages over and above just the minimum wage. Our minimum is too low in many states and it does not cover full cost of survival. However something like 40% of all wage earners do not even earn a minimum wage – and that keeps them in perpetual debt and pushes them to ultra poverty. We must have a much stronger wage vigilance system where principal employers are held accountable for fair / living wages to all workers in their eco-system including contract workers, piece rated workers and workers in the supply chain. The national floor wage must be corrected to at least Rs 500 per day which will then have a cascading effect on state minimum wages. Delhi's example is a good one in this direction.

Urban Employment Guarantee Programme- An urban employment guarantee programme must be put in place and also universally applied. On the lines of NREGA in rural areas, this must create rights based employment in urban areas. This will help protect extended periods of wage-less existence by migrant workers in urban areas during periods of lean absorption. Rajasthan government has announced it in the budget 2022-23 which should be applied to other states as well.

Our public provisioning for migrants in the cities must improve – PDS, health care, housing, transportation etc. Since wages are so low and work is so erratic, publicly provided essentials become really important for survival and even growth. This is how China has grown – but subsidizing essentials like food, housing, health care, education, transportation, it has looked after its workers' basic needs and therefore wages can be low which makes them globally more competitive.

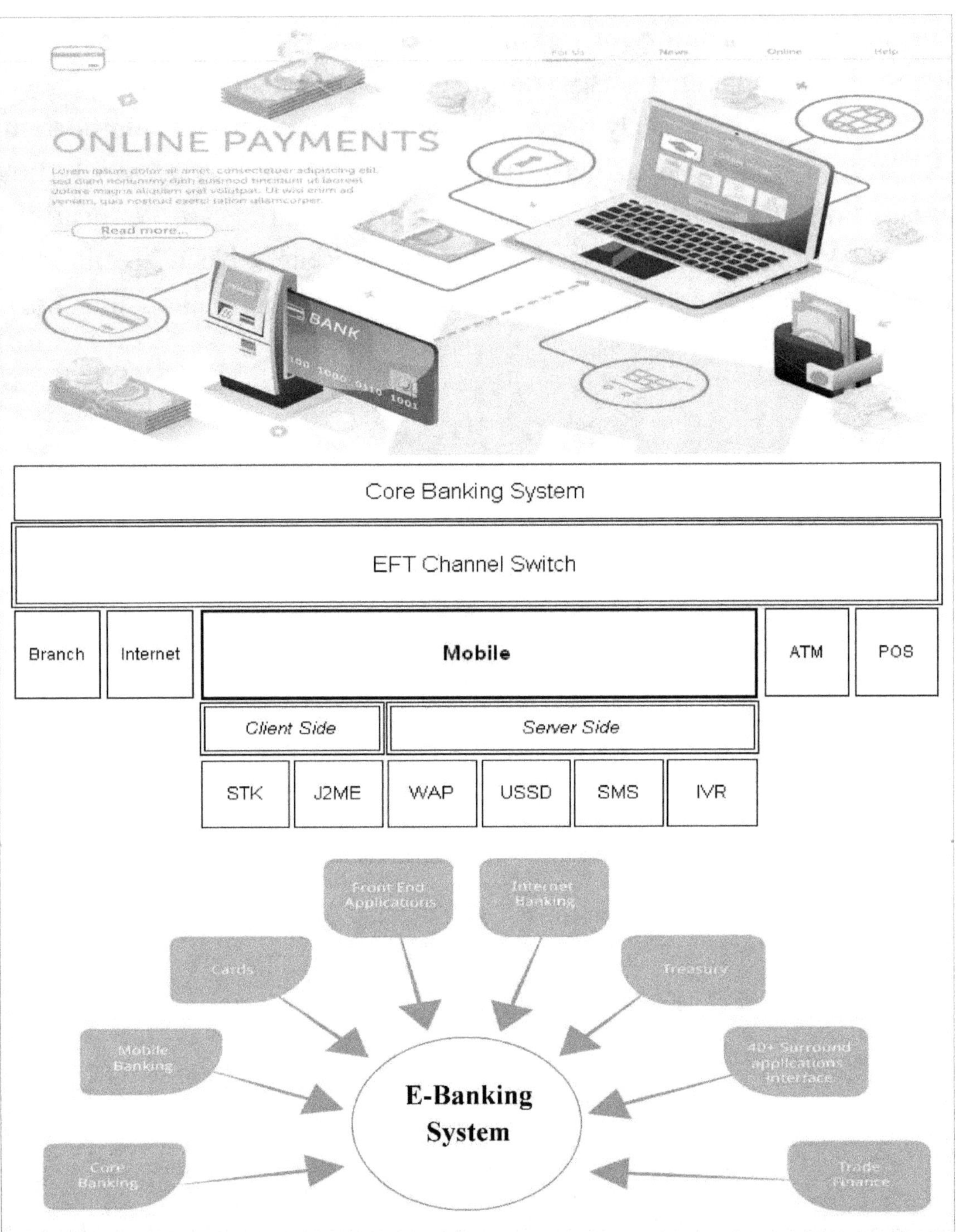

A STUDY ON THE IMPACT OF E-BANKING SYSTEM IN INDIA

Contents

A STUDY ON THE IMPACT OF E-BANKING SYSTEM IN INDIA
ABSTRACT

E-banking plays a pivotal role in the economic growth of a nation. There was a revolution in the banking system with Information and Communication Technology (ICT) and the rapid growth of internet users. Traditional method of banking system is gradually transforming into a virtual banking method. The study will examine the impact of online banking in India and also analyze the trends of e-banking services such as NEFT, RTGS, Mobile Banking and UPI in the country. The study found that there was tremendous growth in all the three e-banking services in the country, which reflects that there was growing awareness of e-banking facilities among the customers and covid-19 gave another thrust to net banking in India.

Keywords: *Online banking, e-banking, digital revolution, ICT, NEFT, RTGS, Mobile Banking and UPI*

Introduction

In India, the digital revolution has led to the surge of internet users in the country. The usage of the internet has gone beyond net surfing and social networking to e-commerce and e-banking. E-banking is also known as online banking or net banking. Electronic banking is a facility offered by the banks as well as financial institutions to their customers that allow them to utilize banking services through internet facilities. Internet has eased work and enhanced efficiency by saving the time and money of people. With e-banking customers are not required to visit their banks to avail the information and services. However, all the services are not available through online banking due to confidential reasons. To avail the online banking services, the customers have to register themselves as they are required a login id and a secret password due to the involvement of high risks of hacking and fraud. Through the online platform, various forms of banking transactions are possible such as online payment, online fund transfer, online shopping and online trading in stocks. It has been found that people who spend most of their time over internet surfing and computers are mostly likely to access e-banking and mobile banking services than non-computer and non-net users (Prema, 2011). Karimzadeh and Alam (2012) found that with the increase in the level of financial literacy and awareness among the people, the usage of net banking in the country has risen. However, the number of net banking users has increased in India after demonetization and further due to covid-19.

Net banking enables financial institutions and bank customers to access their bank accounts, transaction details and information related to financial services like loans, new schemes, mutual funds, fixed deposits. Many commercial banks have eased the opening of savings accounts through e-banking. With net-banking, transactions have become easier internationally. People can trade over the internet, and payment can be made through online banking. Exports and imports become much easier than before. E-banking makes the things possible at your fingertips like online shopping, fund transfer, making e-payments, purchasing financial products like mutual funds, fixed deposits, stock trading, insurance etc. However, it also raises concerns like frauds and hackings. Although the government and other regulatory bodies like RBI have launched fintech start-up services which will keep an eye on any illegal and fraudulent activities and protect the customers. The present study will analyze the impact of online banking on Indian customers, it also shows the advantages and disadvantages of e-banking in India and also analyzed the trends of e-banking services like NEFT, RTGS and Mobile Banking in India.

Definition of e-Banking

Electronic banking is defined as the automated delivery of new and traditional banking products and services directly to the customers through electronic, interactive communication channels (Daniel, 1999). It is nothing but automation of the conventional banking system. It enables the customers to avail the bank products and services digitally i.e. through electronic or online platforms using the internet.

Objectives

1   To study the advantages and dis-advantages of online banking in India.

2   To analyze the impact of e-banking on India.

3   To examine the trends of e-banking services such as NEFT, RTGS and Mobile Banking in India.

Research Methodology and Data Source

The study is descriptive and analytical in nature. The study is based on secondary data collected from various journals, articles, newspaper articles, RBI websites etc. The methodology used is on a year-on-year growth rate and Compound Annual Growth Rate (CAGR) method.

Review of Literature

Kaushik, D. (2019) analyzed the consumer perspective related to net banking versus conventional banking in India. The study attempts to explore the possibilities to blend both the methods of banking. The study spots certain limitations of traditional banking and explores consumer awareness, preferences and satisfaction for e-banking as well as conventional banking.

Suhas and Ramesh (2018) in their study have analyzed the traditional versus online banking methods of operations and found that people are more inclined towards online banking. Their study was mainly focused on the growth of e-banking in India and the products used in the banking sector.

Mukhopadhyay, B. (2016) in his study found that cashless payments have increased significantly in the country with online banking as payments being directly credited into the bank accounts.

Jeon, K. (2014) found that in India, consumers prefer larger banks due to the large number of ATM facilities in the country.

Malhotra, P. and Singh, B. (2010) examines the factors that affect the net banking services in India by using multiple regression models. The study also explored the status of online banking by exploring 82 banks in India. The study found that the private and foreign banks are performing better in online banking services than public sector banks. The study also found that the determining factors are bank size, experience in net banking, financial ownership and pattern which significantly affect the extent of net banking in India.

Uppal, R.K (2010) in his research has found that ATM (Automated Teller Machine) is more effective than mobile banking in the public sector banks. However, mobile banking has played an important role within the net banking and has a positive and significant impact on the net profit of the banks as well as per employee business.

Evolution of e-Banking in India

In 1993, due to the growing need and compulsion, the Government of India adopted computerization in the banking system. The conventional method of banking had overloaded the work of employees, over-crowded branches and long queues outside the bank branches led the Indian Banking Association (IBA) to sign an agreement to computerize the banking system. In 1993, with the recommendations of former RBI Governor C. Rangarajan, computerization of the bank operations was initiated. This was a major breakthrough in the banking system. Further, in 1994, the Saraf Committee recommended extending the practice of Electronic Fund Transfer (EFT), Magnetic Ink Character Recognition (MICR), cheques, and introduction of clearing services electronically beyond the metropolitan cities. Further, in 1996, there was another major breakthrough in banking system i.e., online banking was launched in India by Industrial Credit and Investment Corporation of India (ICICI) bank. This initiative was followed by HDFC Bank, Citibank and IndusInd Bank in 1999. Since then, the Reserve Bank of India has also taken various initiatives for smooth functioning and expansion of net banking in India. Later on the Government of India had passed the IT Act (Information Technology Act) 2000 to legally acknowledge the e-commerce and e-transaction in the country. However, digi-banking became mainstream in the country during 1999 after the reduction of internet charges as well as build-up of trust and awareness about the internet among the people.

According to Deloitte research report, banks should have certain facilities to have fully digital bank such as customizable standing options, order currency options, accounts linked to tax exemptions status, card blocking feature, easily accessible assistance, integration with stock market investment channels, innovation in safety vaults, financial management analytics, enable accounts of different banks merged etc. However, full digitalization is not possible in India due to lack of internet savviness and trust among the people. For certain decisions, interaction between the customers and banks are important to generate trust like during loan requirements and negotiating the terms of loans etc.

Digital Banking, online Banking and E-banking

The Digital Banking definition is banking done through the digital platform, without all the paperwork like cheques, pay-in slips, Demand Drafts and various forms. Digital Banking can be done through a laptop, tablet or mobile phone. Methods of digital banking are Real Time Gross Settlement (RTGS), National Electronic Fund Transfer (NEFT), and National Automated Clearing House (NACH), Electronic Clearing System (ECS), Aadhaar Payments Bridge System (APBS), BHIM Aadhar pay, Card (debit and credit cards) payments, National Electronic Toll Collection (NETC), Unified Payments Interface (UPI), and Immediate payment service (IMPS).

In terms of value of transactions of digital banking, Real Time Gross Settlement (RTGS), National Electronic Fund Transfer (NEFT) are the major players, whereas in terms of volume of transaction, mobile based payments such as Unified Payments Interface (UPI) and Immediate Payment Service (IMPS) are the leaders.

Methods of Digital banking payments

- Real Time Gross Settlement (RTGS)- which can be explained as a system where there is continuous and real-time settlement of fund-transfers, individually on a transaction-by-transaction basis.

- The National Electronic Fund Transfer (NEFT)- payment platform which is used nation-wide by many banks. This allows easy and hassle-free transfer of money from one bank account to another bank account.

- Electronic Clearing System (ECS) is an electronic method of fund transfer from one bank account to another. It is generally used for bulk transfers performed by institutions for making payments like dividend, interest, salary, pension, etc.

- Unified Payments Interface (UPI) - UPI is a virtual payment address (VPA) so the user can transfer funds without entering bank account details or IFSC code. Another feature of UPI is that the applications consolidate all bank accounts in one place. Funds can be transferred and received around the clock. UPI-based apps in India are BHIM, Google Pay, PhonePe. More importantly, UPI-based payments are free of cost.

- National Automated Clearing House (NACH)- National Payments Corporation of India (NPCI) has implemented "National Automated Clearing House (NACH)" for Banks, Financial Institutions, Corporates and Government a web-based solution to facilitate interbank, high volume, electronic transactions which are repetitive and periodic in nature. NACH System can be used for making bulk transactions towards distribution of subsidies, dividends, interest, salary, pension etc. and also for bulk transactions towards collection of payments pertaining to telephone, electricity, water, loans, investments in mutual funds, insurance premium etc.

- Aadhaar Payments Bridge System (APBS) is used for crediting DBT transactions for Government/ Government agency disbursements. DBT aims to transfer subsidies directly to the people through their bank accounts.

- National Electronic Toll Collection (NETC)- National Payments Corporation of India (NPCI) has developed the National Electronic Toll Collection (NETC) program to meet the electronic tolling requirements of the Indian market.

- Immediate payment service (IMPS)- IMPS provides strong & real time fund transfer which offers an instant, 24*7, interbank electronic fund transfer service that could be accessed on multiple channels like Mobile, Internet, ATM, SMS. IMPS allow instant transfer of funds within banks across India which is secure and low cost.

- **Banking cards**- Cards are not only used to withdraw cash but also enable other forms of digital payment. Cards can be used for online transactions and on Point of Sale (PoS) machines. Prepaid cards can also be issued by the banks; such cards are not linked to the bank account but function through the money loaded onto them.

- Unstructured Supplementary Service Data **(USSD)** - By dialing the number *99#, mobile transactions can be carried out without an application and internet connection. The number holds nationwide applicability and promotes greater financial inclusion on the ground level.

- **Mobile Wallets**- Mobile wallets store bank account and card credentials to easily add funds to the wallet and make payments to another person with similar applications. Popular mobile wallets are Paytm, Mobiwik, Freecharge, etc.

- **PoS terminals-** PoS machines are portable devices that read a card to authorize and complete the payment. With digital banking increased, PoS terminals have evolved with virtual and mobile PoS terminals, which makes use of the mobile phone's NFC feature and web-based applications to initiate payment.

Internet and Mobile Banking

The use of electronic and telecommunications networks for delivering various banking products and services. With E-banking, a customer can access his account and operate online transactions using his computer or mobile phone. Electronic banking has many names like e-banking, virtual banking, online banking or internet banking. Generally, banks have websites for different uses of customers, the basic use of e-banking is to provide general information about the bank and its products and services to customers. Another part of the website is related to priority customers to allow customers to conduct transactions on the bank's website. Basic E-banking services are account management, bill payments, new account opening, wire transfers, investment plan, loan application and approval. Other E-banking services are for prioritized customers like account management, cash management, commercial wire transfer, B to B payments, business loan application and approval, business advances, pension plan management, insurance and other portfolio management.

E-banking, internet banking refers to obtaining certain banking services over the internet. Internet banking is a subset of digital banking because internet banking is only limited to core functions. Similarly, mobile banking is availing banking services through mobile-based applications.

Difference between Digital Banking and Online banking or e-Banking

Generally digital banking and online banking are used interchangeably. However, there exists a fine line difference between the meanings of both the terms. Online Banking deals with everyday requirements of customers, like fund transfer, checking balances, loan application to approvals etc. This is the core operation of the bank, which is shifted to online mode with the help of online banking. Online banking is helping hands for both banks as well as customers. Whereas, digital banking is aimed at digitizing all the operations of the bank, basically, starting from account opening form of clients to servicing of the accounts and to the closure of accounts. Digital banking aims to make bank's branch less relevant for customers. Customers can handle all banking operations from their place of convenience. Online banking is a helping hand and bigger part of digital banking.

Why e-Banking is important

Bankers side

i. No paperwork – digital records reduce paperwork and make the process easier to handle. Also, it is environment-friendly.

ii. Less transaction costs – electronic transactions are the cheapest modes of transaction.

iii. A reduced margin for human error – since the information is relayed electronically, there is no room for human error.

iv. More loyal customers – since e-banking services are customer-friendly, banks experience higher loyalty from its customers.

v. Reduced fixed costs – A lesser need for branches which translates into a lower fixed cost.

Customer Side

i. Lower cost per transaction – since the customer does not have to visit the branch for every transaction, it saves him both time and money.

ii. Convenience – a customer can access his account and transact from anywhere 24x7x365.

iii. No geographical barriers – In traditional banking systems, geographical distances could hamper certain banking transactions. However, with e-banking, geographical barriers are reduced.

Business side

i. Low cost – Usually, costs in banking relationships are based on the resources utilized. If a certain business requires more assistance with wire transfers, deposits, etc., then the bank charges it higher fees. With online banking, these expenses are minimized.

ii. Account reviews – Business owners and designated staff members can access the accounts quickly using an online banking interface. This allows them to review the account activity and also ensure the smooth functioning of the account.

iii. Less error – Electronic banking helps reduce errors in regular banking transactions. Bad handwriting, mistaken information, etc. can cause errors which can prove costly. Also, an easy review of the account activity enhances the accuracy of financial transactions.

iv. Better productivity – Electronic banking improves productivity. It allows the automation of regular monthly payments and a host of other features to enhance the productivity of the business.

v. Reduced fraud – Electronic banking provides a digital footprint for all employees who have the right to modify banking activities. Therefore, the business has better visibility into its transactions making it difficult for any fraudsters to play mischief.

Popular Methods of e-Banking

To facilitate mobile payment systems introduced in India with the Mobile Payment Guidelines, 2008 by the Reserve Bank of India to be inter-operable across banks and mobile operators in a safe and secured manner.

There are several methods of E-banking but the most popular and used methods are Immediate payment service (IMPS) and Unified payment interface (UPI).

IMPS and UPI are multichannel and multidimensional platforms that make swift payments possible with required security for even high value transactions.

IMPS provides strong & real time fund transfer which offers an instant, 24*7, interbank electronic fund transfer service that could be accessed on multiple channels like Mobile, Internet, ATM, SMS. IMPS allow instant transfer of funds within banks across India which is secure and low cost. IMPS offer an instant, 24*7 interbank electronic fund transfer service capable of processing person to account, person to person and person to merchant remittances via mobile, internet and ATMs.

Unified Payments Interface (UPI) is a system that powers multiple bank accounts into a single mobile application (of any participating bank), merging several banking features, seamless fund routing & merchant payments into one hood. It also caters to the "Peer to Peer" collect request which can be scheduled and paid as per requirement and convenience.

Characteristics of e-Banking in India

There are certain characteristics of e-banking such as:

- ✓ Check bank statement online.
- ✓ Open a Fixed Deposit schemes.
- ✓ Transfer money to same bank or other bank accounts.
- ✓ Pay bills like mobile post-paid bill, electricity bill, water bill etc.
- ✓ Order cheque books.
- ✓ Purchase insurance policy.
- ✓ Recharge prepaid mobile and DTH services online.
- ✓ Shop online through internet banking.
- ✓ Mobile banking.
- ✓ Cardless payments and withdrawn of money.

Advantages and Disadvantages of e-Banking in India

There are many advantages and disadvantages of online banking.

Advantages of e-Banking

The benefits of e-banking are as follows:

i. **24*7 Services:** The customers can avail banking services 24*7 i.e., 24 hours round the clock throughout the year. The customers can check the account balance/statement and transfer funds anytime without waiting for the bank to open. During this lockdown, when the banking services were almost closed, the customers could utilize the online banking facility without any hiccups.

ii. **Convenience:** Digital banking is more convenient than conventional banking methods. By staying at your office or home the customers can avail the service without standing in a long bank queue which saves travelling time and money.

iii. **Sustainable Development:** One of the important features of e-banking is that we can implement sustainable development in the banking system. Online banking has reduced the paperwork. Customers can view their account statement online which saves lots of paper and saves the trees.

iv. **Easy to operate:** Net banking is simple and easy. If the customers are technology savvy, banking is at the tip of their finger. Anyone can easily learn how to operate it.

v. **Efficiency:** E-banking is more efficient than traditional methods as the transactions can be completed within a few minutes via online banking. Money can be transferred to any bank account within the country in a few minutes and customers can also open Fixed Deposits easily.

vi. **Transaction Tracker:** All the transactions the customers made through e-banking are recorded in the online portal of the bank which can act as a proof if required. The details of the online fund transfers like payee's name; account details like account number, bank name, IFSC code, Branch and State; date and time of payment etc. are recorded which in conventional banking is available through acknowledgment but we can lose them any time.

vii. **Online Shopping:** Nowadays, instead of visiting the crowded market and wasting time, people prefer online shopping where they get a variety of goods by sitting at their home. During this pandemic, online shopping, especially the grocery items and basic necessities goods has become necessary. People instead of going outside due to corona and lockdown, ordered online goods. However, for online shopping you need a bank account to make the transactions. Therefore, this eases the shopping at your doorsteps.

viii. **Automatic Payment Options:** Customers can pay the utility bills such as electricity, water, post-paid mobile, gas and credit cards regularly by selecting the automatic payment options. Nowadays, with busy schedules, customers forget the due dates to make the regular payments. This option has warded off the concerns of the customers to pay the utility bills without any miss.

Disadvantages of e-Banking

Online banking is not free from drawbacks. Following are the drawbacks:

i. **Uninterrupted Internet Facility:** For online banking you need high-speed, uninterrupted internet facility else your transaction will either fail or it might hang in between. People staying in remote areas or poor internet facilities will face problems with e-banking. Though if the server of the bank is down then the facility will be disrupted.

ii. **Security Issues:** E-banking involves lots of transaction risk. Despite advanced encryption methods to protect the data of the customers, there are lots of cases of cybercrimes which the police and government are unable to crack down. People with less knowledge about it fall into the trap of the hackers and lose their money. Precautions should be taken by the banks but hackers are smarter than the bank authorities and government.

iii. **Problem with Non-Tech savvy customers**: People with poor or no technological knowledge are unable to surf the internet and hence online banking and transactions are difficult to operate. Countries like India, where a large section of the people is uneducated and staying in rural areas are unable to do online banking. They find traditional methods safer and easier.

Impact of e-Banking in India

The Covid-19 pandemic has given a big thrust to online banking in the country. People have kept pace with fast-changing technology, and adopted new technology. Banking sector have focused on facilitating digital penetration, variety of payment systems to build the objective of a "less-cash" society. Efforts were also taken for smooth functioning of all the payment systems. Keeping in mind social-distancing and no physical contact, people welcomed digital payments.

Digital technology plays an important role in enhancing financial inclusion and thereby contributing to economic growth of the country. But the use of digital banking services depends on either awareness or proper information regarding various services among the people.

In September 2020, there was a surge of e-banking and m-banking (mobile banking) in the country with 80.7 million net-banking users (that is 22 percent higher than previous year) and 18.3 million m-banking users (that is 20 percent higher than 2019) was been recorded in the country.

The following section shows the growth and share in and volume and value of various digital banking payments methods in India from 2015 to 2021.

Volume of Transactions through different modes of Payments System

The volume of transactions in digital banking is shown in the below table and diagram for the time period 2015 to 2021.

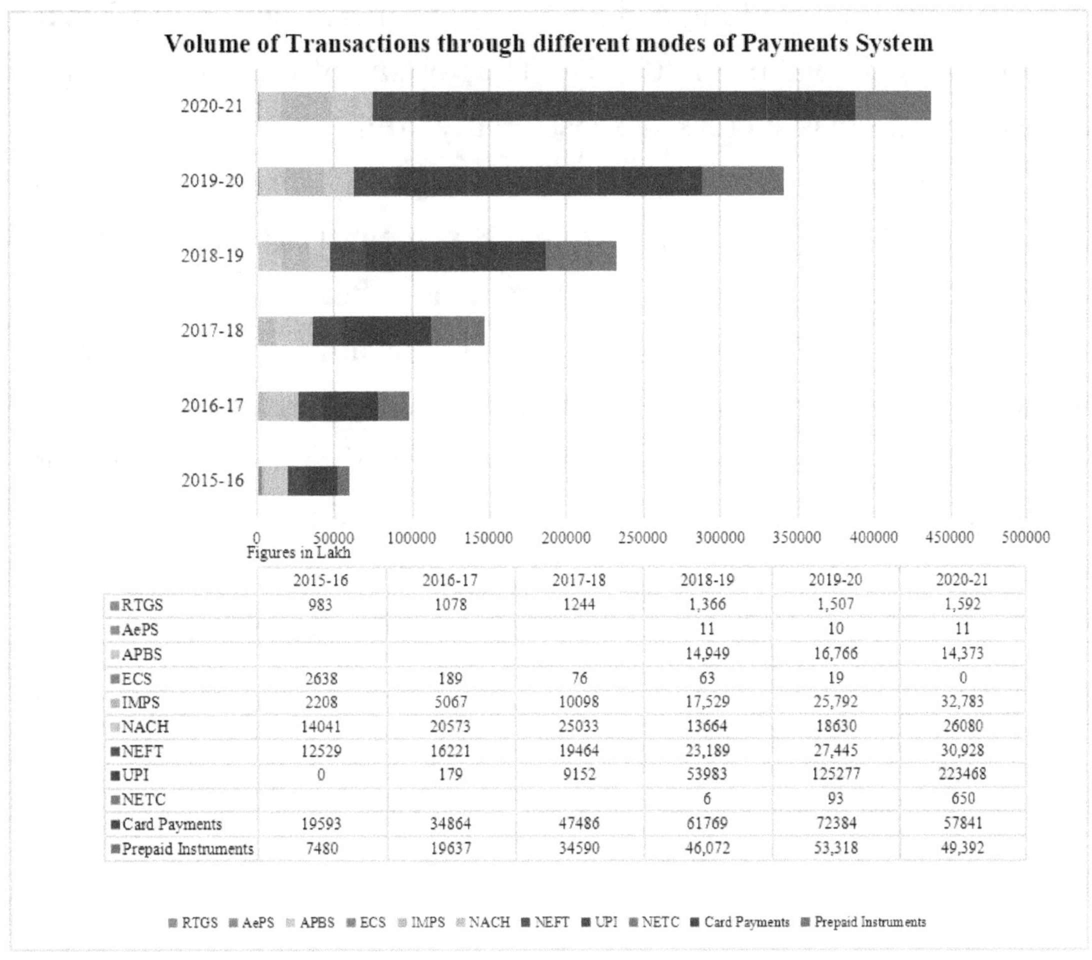

	2015-16	2016-17	2017-18	2018-19	2019-20	2020-21
RTGS	983	1078	1244	1,366	1,507	1,592
AePS				11	10	11
APBS				14,949	16,766	14,373
ECS	2638	189	76	63	19	0
IMPS	2208	5067	10098	17,529	25,792	32,783
NACH	14041	20573	25033	13664	18630	26080
NEFT	12529	16221	19464	23,189	27,445	30,928
UPI	0	179	9152	53983	125277	223468
NETC				6	93	650
Card Payments	19593	34864	47486	61769	72384	57841
Prepaid Instruments	7480	19637	34590	46,072	53,318	49,392

There is a tremendous rise in the volume of transactions of IMPS, UPI and pre-paid instruments. IMPS rose from 2,208 lakhs in 2015-16 to 32,783 lakhs in 2020-21 which increased by almost 15 times during the period. In the same time UPI showed a steep rise from 179 lakhs in 2016-17 to 2,23,468 lakhs in 2020-21 which registered an increase by almost 1248 times during the period. After 2018-19, there is a steep rise in mobile banking transactions. NEFT volume of transactions recorded moderate improvement from 12529 lakh in 2015-16 to 30928 lakh in 2020-21. The volume of transactions in RTGS has not increased much compared to mobile banking and NEFT. It has increased from 983 lakhs in 2015-16 to 1592 lakhs in 2020-21. The volume of translations in pre-paid instruments has increased substantially from 7480 lakh to 49,392 lakh from the 2015-16 to 2020-21 but marginally down compared to 2019-20 of 53318 lakh which is around 8 percent. Card payments have the second highest volume of transitions after UPI. Volume of transactions from 2015-16 to 2019-20 show upward trends from 19,593 lakh to 72,384 lakh but in 2020-21 it drastically decreased to 57,841 which is around 25 per cent. The lower volume of transactions in AePS is around 11 lakh and zero in ECS. NACH volume of transactions recorded improvement from 14041 lakh in 2015-16 to 25033 lakh in 2017-18, submissive in 2018-19 and 2019-20 and reached to 26080 lakhs in 2020-21.

Volume of Transactions through different modes of Payments System- Percentage Share of payment modes

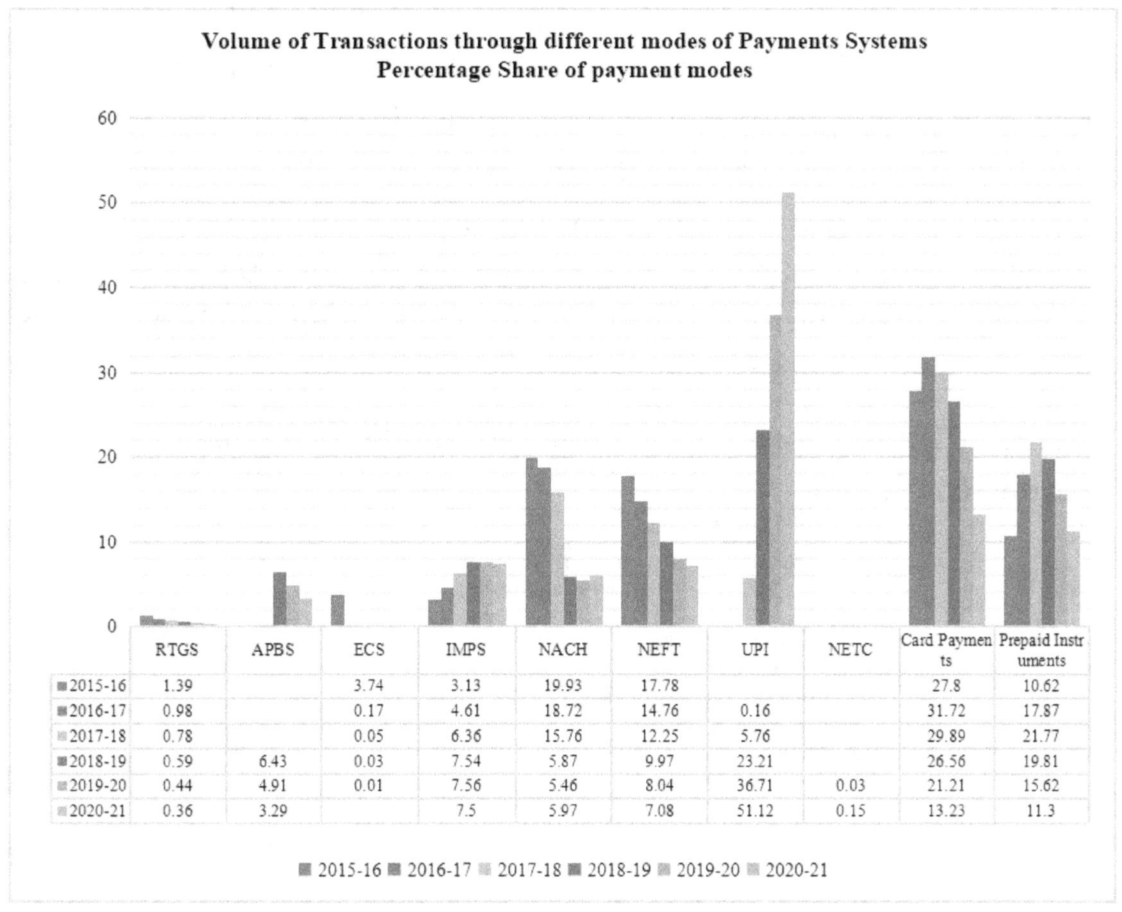

	RTGS	APBS	ECS	IMPS	NACH	NEFT	UPI	NETC	Card Payments	Prepaid Instruments
2015-16	1.39		3.74	3.13	19.93	17.78			27.8	10.62
2016-17	0.98		0.17	4.61	18.72	14.76	0.16		31.72	17.87
2017-18	0.78		0.05	6.36	15.76	12.25	5.76		29.89	21.77
2018-19	0.59	6.43	0.03	7.54	5.87	9.97	23.21		26.56	19.81
2019-20	0.44	4.91	0.01	7.56	5.46	8.04	36.71	0.03	21.21	15.62
2020-21	0.36	3.29		7.5	5.97	7.08	51.12	0.15	13.23	11.3

From the above graph, it is clear that percentage share in total volume of transaction RTGS, NACH and NEFT in 2015-16 to 2020-21 went downward from 1.39 percent to 0.36 percent, 19.93 percent to 5.9 percent and 17.78 to 7.08 percent respectively. Whereas UPI and IMPS showed an upward trend from 0.16 percent to 51.12 percent and 3.13 percent to 7.5 percent respectively.

ECS shows a downward trend from 3.74 percent in 2015-16 to 0.01 percent 2019-20. Card payments have also come down from 27.8 percent in 2015-16 to 13.23 percent in 2020-21. NETC introduced in

2019-20 has risen to 0.15 percent in 2020-21. Prepaid instruments, like smart card, online wallets, mobile wallets etc., percentage share in total volume of transaction was 10.62 percent in 2015-16. It increased to 21.77 percent in 2017-18 and came down to 11.3 percent in 2020-21. In percentage share of different mode of payment, 2018-19 is a path breaking year. From 2015-16 to 2018-19 RTGS, NEFT, Card payments and prepaid instruments are either stable in percentage of volume of transaction share or increasing trends but after 2018-19 the percentage share were shrinking and simultaneously UPI and IMPS gained momentum in the volume of transaction share.

Volume of Transactions through different modes of Payments System-Year on Year growth

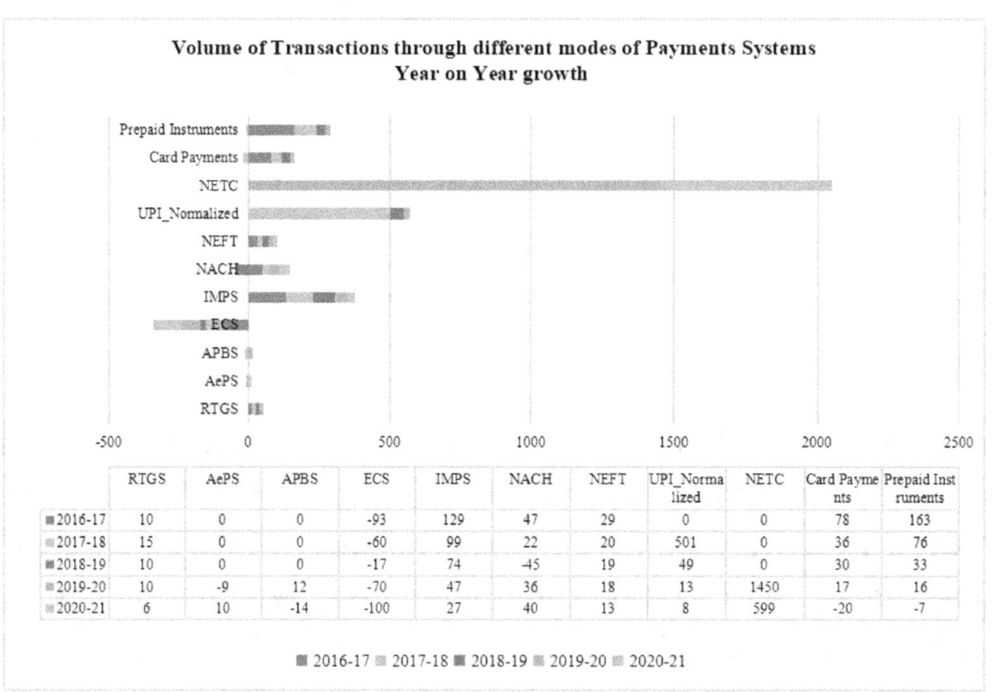

	RTGS	AePS	APBS	ECS	IMPS	NACH	NEFT	UPI_Normalized	NETC	Card Payments	Prepaid Instruments
2016-17	10	0	0	-93	129	47	29	0	0	78	163
2017-18	15	0	0	-60	99	22	20	501	0	36	76
2018-19	10	0	0	-17	74	-45	19	49	0	30	33
2019-20	10	-9	12	-70	47	36	18	13	1450	17	16
2020-21	6	10	-14	-100	27	40	13	8	599	-20	-7

From the above graphic, it is clear that the YoY growth in total volume of transaction, ECS is clearly on the negative side. RTGS and NEFT also reflect moderate growth but on the downward side. While NACH growth is almost constant in all the years. Whereas UPI and IMPS and NETC show vibrant growth with a lot of fluctuations in upward trends. Card payments, prepaid instruments and APBS have shown negative growth for the period 2020-21.

Value of Transactions through different modes of Payments System

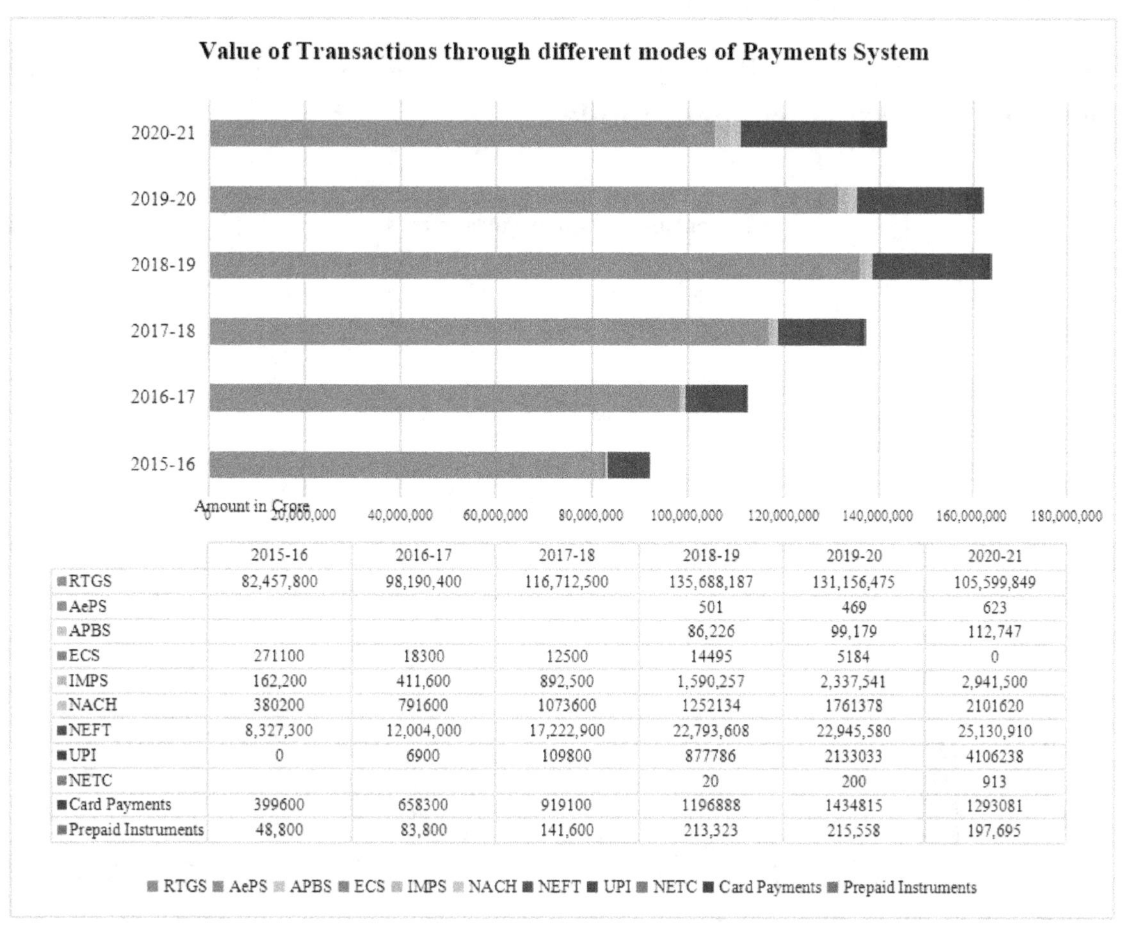

	2015-16	2016-17	2017-18	2018-19	2019-20	2020-21
RTGS	82,457,800	98,190,400	116,712,500	135,688,187	131,156,475	105,599,849
AePS				501	469	623
APBS				86,226	99,179	112,747
ECS	271100	18300	12500	14495	5184	0
IMPS	162,200	411,600	892,500	1,590,257	2,337,541	2,941,500
NACH	380200	791600	1073600	1252134	1761378	2101620
NEFT	8,327,300	12,004,000	17,222,900	22,793,608	22,945,580	25,130,910
UPI	0	6900	109800	877786	2133033	4106238
NETC				20	200	913
Card Payments	399600	658300	919100	1196888	1434815	1293081
Prepaid Instruments	48,800	83,800	141,600	213,323	215,558	197,695

From the above graph, it is clear that with regards to the value of transactions through different modes of digital banking, the value of the amount of RTGS is the greatest when compared to other methods of payments. The value of the amount in RTGS is ₹ 82,457,800 crore in 2015 and ₹ 105,599,849 crore in 2021. The amount value of NEFT is ₹ 8,327,300 crore in 2015 and ₹ 25,130,910 crore in 2021.

In the same time, UPI showed a steep rise from 6900 crore in 2016 to 41,06,238 crore in 2021 which registered an increase by almost 595 times during the period. IMPS value of transactions recorded a steep rise during 2015 to 2021 which is 1,62,200 crores to 29,41,500 crore. NACH value transactions gained moderate improvement from 3,80,200 crore in 2015 to 21,01,620 crore in 2021.

Value of Transactions through different modes of Payments System- Percentage Share of payment modes

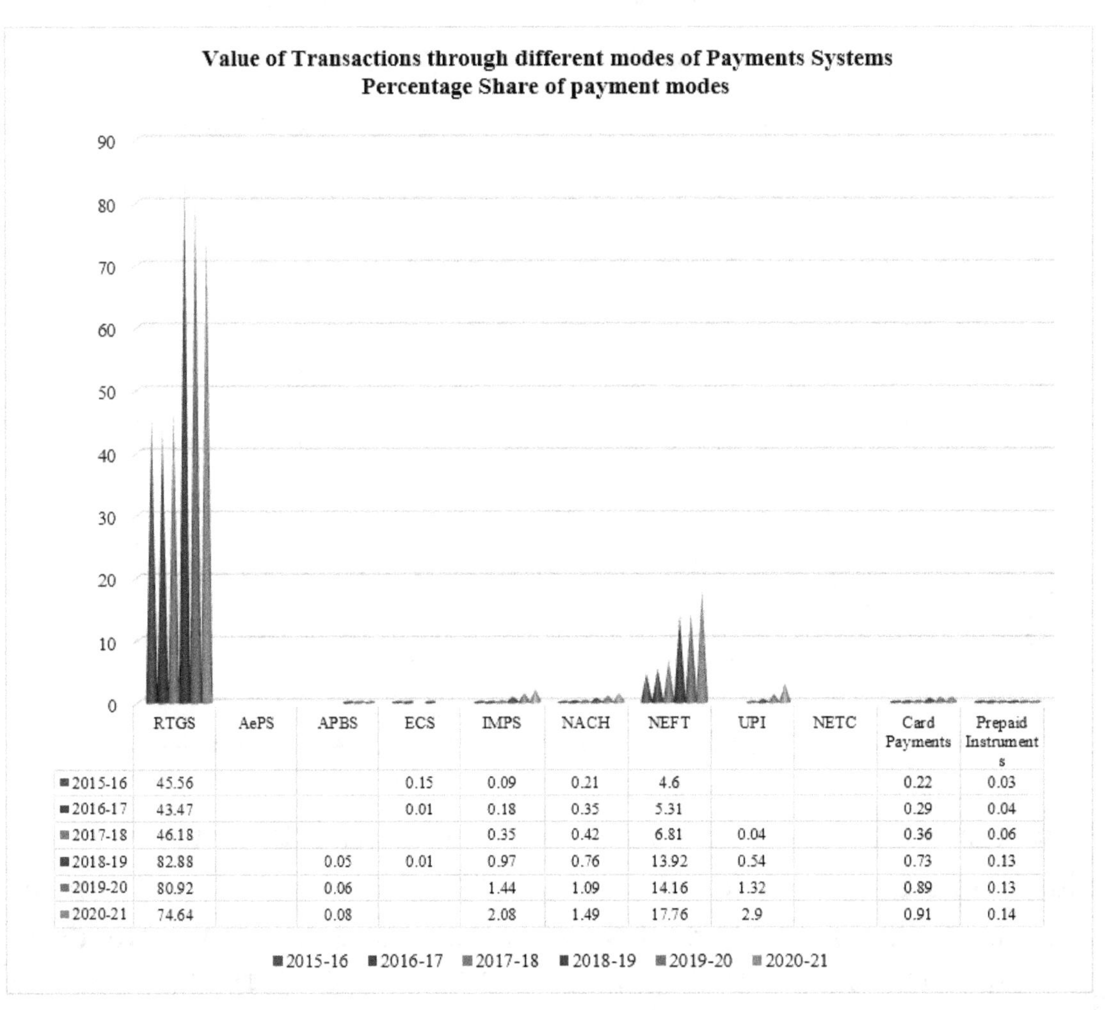

	RTGS	AePS	APBS	ECS	IMPS	NACH	NEFT	UPI	NETC	Card Payments	Prepaid Instruments
2015-16	45.56			0.15	0.09	0.21	4.6			0.22	0.03
2016-17	43.47			0.01	0.18	0.35	5.31			0.29	0.04
2017-18	46.18				0.35	0.42	6.81	0.04		0.36	0.06
2018-19	82.88		0.05	0.01	0.97	0.76	13.92	0.54		0.73	0.13
2019-20	80.92		0.06		1.44	1.09	14.16	1.32		0.89	0.13
2020-21	74.64		0.08		2.08	1.49	17.76	2.9		0.91	0.14

From the above graph, it is clear that percentage share in total value of transaction of RTGS is on upward trend from 45.56 percent in 2015-16 to 82.88 percent in 2018-19, from 2018-19 the value transaction of RTGS declined to 74.64 percent in 2020-21. The NACH and NEFT in 2015-16 to 2020-21 was upward trend from 0.21 percent to 1.49 percent, 4.6 percent to 17.76 percent respectively. Whereas UPI and IMPS shows upward side trends, IMPS increased from 0.09 percent in 2015-16 to 2.08 percent in 2020-21, whereas UPI percentage share dramatically increased from 0.04 percent in 2018-19 to 2.9 percent in 2020-21. ECS shows a downward trend from 015 percent in 2015-16 to no transaction in 2020-21.

Value of Transactions through different modes of Payments System-Year on Year growth

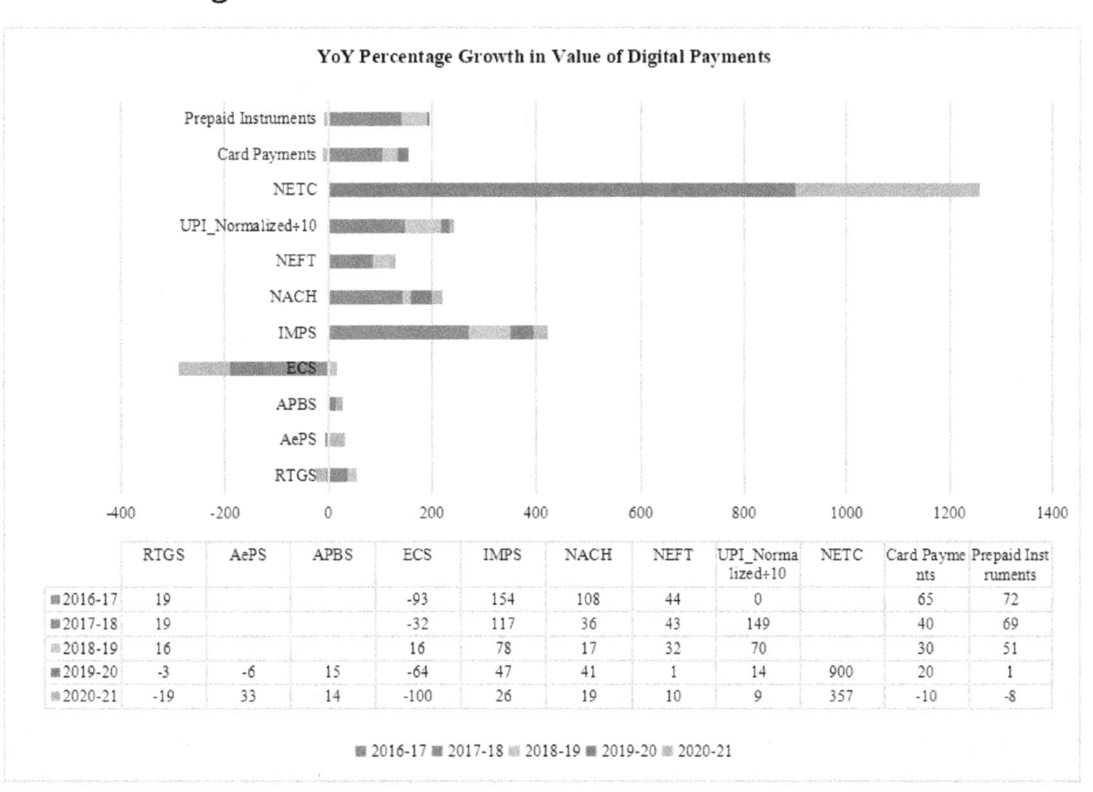

	RTGS	AePS	APBS	ECS	IMPS	NACH	NEFT	UPI_Normalized+10	NETC	Card Payments	Prepaid Instruments
2016-17	19			-93	154	108	44	0		65	72
2017-18	19			-32	117	36	43	149		40	69
2018-19	16			16	78	17	32	70		30	51
2019-20	-3	-6	15	-64	47	41	1	14	900	20	1
2020-21	-19	33	14	-100	26	19	10	9	357	-10	-8

From the above graph, it is clear that the YoY growth in total value of transaction, ECS clearly is on the negative side. RTGS shows negative growth in 2019-20 and 2020-21. NEFT and NACH reflect moderate growth. Whereas UPI and IMPS and NETC show vibrant growth with a lot of fluctuations in upward trends. Card payments, prepaid instruments and APBS have shown negative growth for the period 2020-21.

Value of per transactions through different modes of payments- Year on Year growth

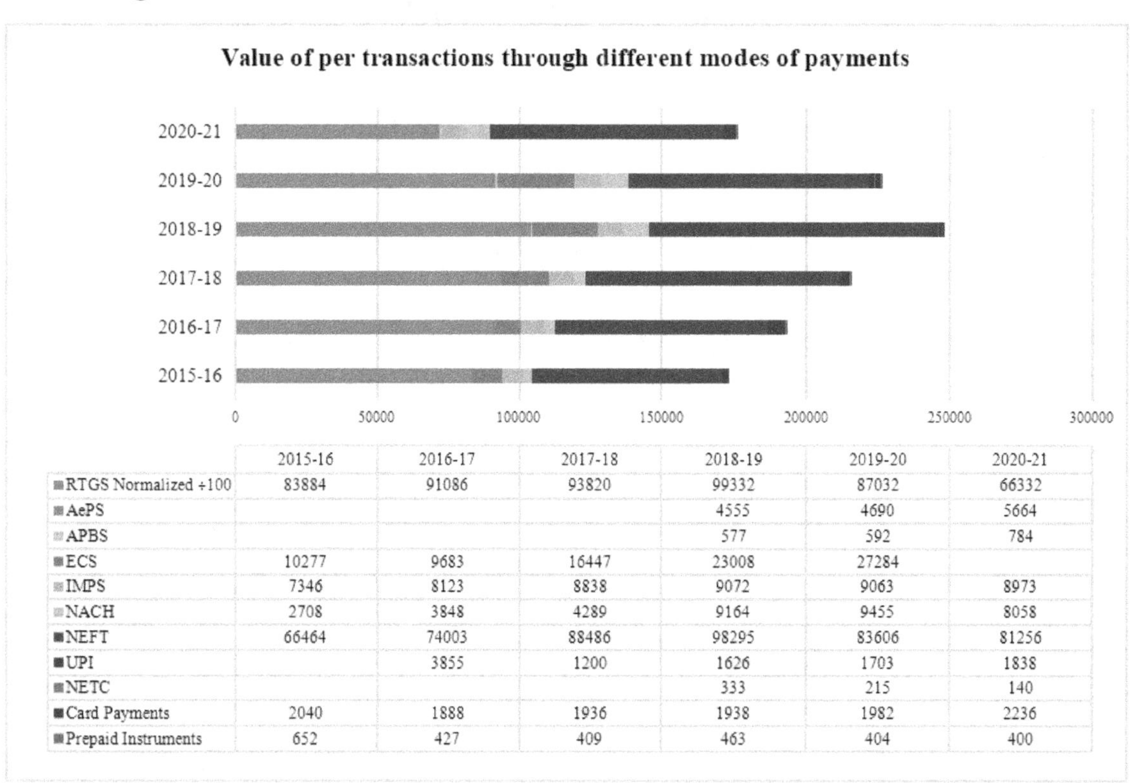

	2015-16	2016-17	2017-18	2018-19	2019-20	2020-21
RTGS Normalized ÷100	83884	91086	93820	99332	87032	66332
AePS				4555	4690	5664
APBS				577	592	784
ECS	10277	9683	16447	23008	27284	
IMPS	7346	8123	8838	9072	9063	8973
NACH	2708	3848	4289	9164	9455	8058
NEFT	66464	74003	88486	98295	83606	81256
UPI		3855	1200	1626	1703	1838
NETC				333	215	140
Card Payments	2040	1888	1936	1938	1982	2236
Prepaid Instruments	652	427	409	463	404	400

From the above table, the value of per transactions through different modes of payments is given. The value per transaction for RTGS has increased from Rs. 8,38,84,000 in 2015-16 to Rs 9,93,32,000 in 2018-19. After 2018-19 per transaction value of RTGS has drastically gone down and reached to Rs. 6,63,32,000. This decline in value of RTGS is due to gloomy economic activity and rapid increase of other modes of payments. The NEFT value has an upward trend from Rs. 66,464 in 2015-16 to Rs. 81,256 in 2020-21. The growth in the value of card payments is more or less stable to around Rs. 2000. NACH value per transaction has increased its highest from Rs. 2708 in 2015-16 to Rs. 9455 2019-20. ECS, AcPS, APBS, ECS & IMPS have increased in their per value transactions. The value of per transactions of UPI & prepaid has decreased to Rs 1838 and Rs 400 in 2020-21 from Rs 2016-17 and Rs 652 in 2015-16 respectively.

Conclusions

The above analysis revealed that from 2015-16 to 2018-19 traditional payments systems like RTGS, NEFT, Card payments, prepaid instruments etc. were on upward or stable trends with respect to volume, value or per transaction value but after 2018-19, the percentage share and YoY growth were shrinking in the above mentioned payment systems and simultaneously mobile based payment instruments such as UPI, IMPS NETC gained weight in volume of transaction, value of transaction and per transaction value. The growing relevance of e-banking is due to digital revolution and surge of internet users in the country. The study reveals that covid-19 pandemic has given another biggest thrust to online banking in the country. Due to uncertain lockdown people make their transactions through online and therefore, there was a tremendous surge of e-banking users in 2020-21 within the country. The study concludes that easy and affordable internet access with cheap smartphone benefited the e-banking ecosystem. The lockdown due to covid-19 has also boosted the e-banking facilities in the country.

References

- Daniel, E. (1999). "Provision of electronic banking in the UK and the Republic of Ireland", International Journal of Bank Marketing, 1999;17(2):72-82.

- Jeon, K. (2014). "Essays on banking industry: ATM (Automatic Teller Machine)".

- Karimzadeh M. and Alam D. (2012). "Electronic banking challenges in India: An empirical investigation", Interdisciplinary Journal of Contemporary Research in Business, Vol. 4 No. 2, pp. 31-45

- Kaushik, D. (2019). "A Study of Internet-Banking in Financial Development in India", *Journal of Advances and Scholarly Researches in Allied Education*, Volume: 16 / Issue: 2, pg: 108 - 114 (7), E-ISSN: 2230-7540

- Malhotra, P. and Singh, B. (2010). "An analysis of Internet banking offerings and its determinants in India", Internet Research 20(1):87-106. DOI:10.1108/10662241011020851

- Prema, C. (2011). "A framework for understanding consumer perceived characteristics of internet banking as predictors of its adoption", Indian Journal of Marketing, Vol. 41, No. 2: pp. 46-53.

- RBI Annual Reports- payment and settlement systems and information technology

- Statista 2021. Number of mobile banking payments across India from financial year 2013 to 2019. Retrieved from https://www.statista.com/statistics/870487/india-mobile-banking-payment-volume/

- Suhas. D. and, Ramesh, H. N. (2018). "E-banking and its growth in India – A synoptic view", Journal of Management Research and Analysis, October-December, 2018;5(4):376-383

- Uppal, R. K. (2010). "Emerging issues and strategies to enhance M-banking services", African Journal of Marketing Mana